The Wise
Inheritor

The Wise Inheritor

> *Protecting, Preserving,*
> *and Enjoying*
> *Your Legacy*

ANN PERRY

Broadway Books New York

This book is intended for informational purposes only and is not meant to take the place of legal advice. The laws in this area are complex and constantly changing. You should consult with an experienced attorney to apply the relevant laws in your state to your unique situation.

The author has changed the names of some of the people described in the book in order to protect their privacy. Any resulting resemblance to persons living or dead is entirely coincidental and unintentional.

BROADWAY

Broadway Books titles may be purchased for business or promotional use or for special sales. For information, please write to: Special Markets Department, Random House, Inc., 280 Park Avenue, New York, NY 10017.

PRINTED IN THE UNITED STATES OF AMERICA

BROADWAY BOOKS and its logo, a letter B bisected on the diagonal, are trademarks of Broadway Books, a division of Random House, Inc.

Visit our website at www.broadwaybooks.com

Book design by Chris Welch.

Library of Congress Cataloging-in-Publication Data
Perry, Ann, 1953–
The wise inheritor: protecting, preserving, and
enjoying your legacy / Ann Perry.
p. cm.
Includes index.
ISBN 0-7679-0835-X
1. Finance, Personal. 2. Inheritance and succession. 3. Estate planning.
I. Title.
HG179.P3667 2003
332.024'01—dc21
2002026010

Dedicated with love to my husband, Tony,
and to our sons, Wes and Mike,
who have given me much more than
I could ever leave them.

Contents

Acknowledgments

Special thanks for friendship and encouragement to Janet Lowe, Peg Eddy, Susan Erman, and Elizabeth Douglass.

For professional expertise and assistance, I thank Mark Dowling, Nancy A. Spector, Jean Sinclair, Henry E. Zapisek, Curt Welker, Russell Griffith, James Miller, Richard J. Muscio, Valerie Jacobs, Michael Stolper, John J. Levy, Mary Clarno, Joan Cudhea, Steve Carter, Sheryl Rowling, J. Steven Cowen, Les Merrithew, Jeanne Bradford-Odorico, Neil Hokanson, Candace Bahr, Ginita Wall, Thomas Warschauer, Jim Vauth, and Olivia Mellan.

Thanks to my fellow writers for their encouragement, Sylvia Tiersten, Dale Fetherling, and Beverly Trainer, and also to *San Diego Union-Tribune* business editors Jim Watters and Laura Coffey.

I owe particular gratitude to my agent, Colleen

Mohyde, for her patience and unfailing graciousness, and a thank-you to Bob Veres for introducing us. At Broadway Books, my editor, Patricia Medved, displayed a marvelous knack for deftness and humor, as well as great insight.

And finally, thanks to the inheritors who generously shared their personal experiences with me.

Introduction

Becoming the Go Fish Heiress

When my husband and I bought our first house in 1981, we were able to draw upon an unusual source to help make the down payment. My late grandmother, a writer and inventor of children's games, left a small legacy—the rights to the first mass-marketed "Go Fish" card game. Introduced in the 1950s, the small fish-shaped cards designed to fit in the hands of young children provided her, and eventually my father and mother, with several thousand dollars annual income for many years.

My mother thought it a fitting legacy that some of the Go Fish money help us get a start. When friends marveled that my husband and I had bought a house in pricey Southern California in the midst of a recession and record-high interest rates, my husband would respond with a straight face, "My wife is the Go Fish heiress."

Of course, the joke was that no one would ever con-
fuse me with an heiress. My father sold printing products
and my mother taught third grade. They both drove sec-
ondhand cars that often broke down in the desert heat of
El Paso, Texas. Both my husband and I came from solidly
middle-class families. His father was a machinist and his
mother worked as a nurse to put him through college.
In the early 1980s, we were newly married, working as
newspaper reporters and thrilled that we were making the
monthly installments on a home in the suburbs. The Go
Fish money was the perfect sort of windfall, welcome
help from an elderly relative who had lived far away and
whom I had seen only occasionally.

The Next Inheritance

Within ten years, however, I would be faced with inheriting all that my grandparents and parents had
accumulated. In 1993, when my mother died at age
seventy-four, I became one of the first in the wave of
baby boomers to grapple with the bequests of their World
War II–era parents. (My father had died in 1976.) This
was a much more painful and complicated windfall.

My mother had thoughtfully prepared a will leaving
me, as an only child, all her possessions. She had even
handed me a list of her assets handwritten on a yellow
sheet of legal paper—bank accounts, stocks, IRAs, with
their estimated values and where they could be found.
Although her actions clearly said, "Here, I'm giving you
everything I own. Use and enjoy," I felt whipsawed be-

tween guilt and elation. The sum of my parents' modest life when liquidated would be worth at least $500,000.

During many of the eighteen months my mother was terminally ill, I struggled to care for her in our home, while also caring for my two young sons ages five and one, working, and trying to find time for my husband. Every day was an exhausting one. And the thought of coping with my impending inheritance was sometimes overwhelming. I can still remember driving home from work one afternoon and suddenly realizing what her possessions added to my own family's would mean: Two cats, three houses, four cars and five television sets. That's too much! I can't handle it! I was beginning to experience, as have many other heirs, the emotional burden that comes with inheritance.

And all too soon, those things *were* mine. My net worth had just quintupled, but I was far from happy. My two young sons would never really know my parents or my family home. I couldn't call up my mother for tips on making homemade pie crust or a good laugh over the toddler who decorated the living room couch with a Hershey's squeeze bottle. Certainly, I was relieved to have some greater financial security for our family, but at the same time I was bereft, a thirty-nine-year-old orphan. I felt thrust into a new stage of adult life, where I was to get on-the-job training in managing a scary sum of assets.

My inheritance included: the family home in El Paso; a 1913 summer house on Lake Michigan that my father's father purchased in 1933; bank certificates of deposit; shares of Exxon, Central & Southwest, and Bell South; an old English painting; a $30,000 IRA; stock in a mysterious Canadian mining company; lots of old books; the rights to the Go Fish game; and a black cat named Sarah Jane.

The Emotional Challenges

At least, I told myself, once I get past the grieving I'll know how to handle this estate. After seven years as a general business writer with the San Diego newspaper, I had recently been named the personal finance columnist. I told myself, I'll learn just what to do with my mother's IRA, the family Exxon stock, and the summer cabin. Well, I was wrong on two counts. First, grieving isn't necessarily something you get over quickly. And second, knowing what to do with your finances and following through on that know-how are two different things.

I kept bumping up against my emotions as I tried to deal rationally with the assets I'd inherited. While I could write in my column that it's generally best not to have more than 10 percent of your investment assets in any one company, I found the prospect of selling most of my $130,000 in Exxon stock for diversification a frightening prospect. The stock gave me a feeling of safety and protection, as if my family were still watching over me. And I felt an odd sort of loyalty to the stock. Look how good it had been to my family.

I knew, too, that it wasn't smart to let my mother's house in El Paso, the family home since I was five, sit there month after month continuing to accumulate tax and utility bills. But I was frozen with indecision. When my accountant, logically, asked why I didn't rent it out, I recoiled as if he'd suggested renting out room in a mausoleum. I just shook my head. I couldn't bear the thought of anyone else living there.

It began to dawn on me that I couldn't discuss the "problems" I encountered managing an estate with just anyone. It's not a good idea to let drop that you've just had a big bump-up in wealth around the office, at the PTA social, or with most people who knew you pre-bequest. I worried that people might envy or criticize me. Just as people are quick to judge on appearances and first impressions, so too are they likely to judge you by your perceived economic station.

At work I dealt all day long with the subject of money, yet I couldn't share my good financial fortune with anyone except my husband, my accountant, and my estate planning attorney. It was liberating finally when I made a friend of a woman who'd come into an inheritance the same time I had. We discussed the challenges and complications with the silent understanding neither would ever "out" the other in our social group.

The Inheritance Taboo

The more I wrote and thought about how people manage their money, the more I realized that inheritance is a particularly isolating event. Inheritors can find themselves suddenly at odds with siblings and spouses over the bequest. It's often said, correctly I believe, that money is the last taboo—that people are more likely to tell you how many times a week they have sex than they are to confess their net worth. But I think of inheritance as a triple taboo—at the intersection of three emotionally charged issues: money, death, and family relations.

Inherited money isn't like other money. You didn't earn it, save it, or invest it. You received it because someone—probably someone for whom you cared—died. That's why your feelings about an inheritance can be conflicted and confused. Getting an inheritance is not at all like winning the lottery or striking it rich with company stock options, as some have suggested. The lottery, of course, is just a matter of luck. And starting or working at a successful company requires some initiative. Even the lowliest engineer at a high-tech company who makes millions from stock options can say: I might be fortunate, but I earned it, I worked hard, I took on risk in choosing to work for this company over others. If these newly rich feel guilty, it stems more from the feeling that they have so much when others—including family and friends—have much less.

When I surveyed the books written for inheritors, I found several, the most popular containing solid financial and legal advice. But they were not written from the perspective of the heirs. Inheritors need more than just good advice. They need, first of all, to know they are not alone in treating inherited money differently from other money. They need an understanding of why they feel deeply about what they've inherited, how this affects their behavior, and what they can do to improve their financial security. That's when I decided to write this book—combining my personal experience and that of other inheritors with my decade-long work as a financial writer. I wanted to acknowledge and understand the emotions that heirs feel so they could better manage their new wealth.

Researchers predict that a mere 1 percent of the nation's baby boomers will get one-third of all the wealth passed from the World War II generation. This book, however, is not just for them. It's for anyone who views an inheritance as a problem or an opportunity, or both. A modest bequest, if managed well, can make a huge difference in the life of the inheritor.

Even a Modest Bequest Matters

Looking back now as an adult, I can see that the small inheritance of $1,000 that my mother received from her parents in the late 1950s marked a turning point in our lives. At a time when my parents were struggling financially, it bootstrapped us into middle class. My mother used the money to make a down payment on a $13,000 two-bedroom house. Up until then, we had been living in a rented house for married graduate students at the nearby university. The "yard" consisted of dirt and hardscrabble rock outcroppings. The new house, on the other hand, had trees and a backyard with a lawn. The front opened out to a large green park. It was my parents' first and only home.

My husband's parents, who died several years after my mother, left an estate of roughly the same size, or about

$500,000. Some $300,000 of that came from the sale of their comfortable two-bedroom home in the San Francisco Bay Area where prices had skyrocketed with the explosion of high-tech companies. The rest came from their savings. My husband and his brother each received about $250,000.

As the inheritances that my husband and I received illustrate, middle-class families can leave good-sized estates. Since the 1980s, two key assets have shown substantial growth: real estate and stocks. It's not uncommon for older Americans to own a home with several hundred thousand dollars in equity, a respectable portfolio of stocks, and life insurance. An estate of half a million, one million, or more is commonplace. And of course, some heirs will receive more than one inheritance. Many inheritors have told me they were surprised how much their parents, aunts, and uncles and other relatives had accumulated. One woman marveled, "Dad didn't even realize it. He was almost a millionaire."

Do Like the Rich: Hold On to It

When I think about what my parents left me, I'm amazed and gratified by their tenacity. The most valuable assets—the cabin in Michigan, the Exxon stock—passed from my grandparents to my parents and then to me. These didn't get sold to pay off a pressing bill or to buy a new car. In their own middle-class way, my parents were doing what rich family dynasties have long practiced: creating wealth for future generations. Talking about my long-term holdings one day with San Diego money manager Mark Dowling, he joked that I'd discovered the ultimate "hot tip" to stock market success: "Pssst!! Buy Exxon and hold it for fifty years!" As more and more Americans, and not just the upper class, accumulate valuable assets that can be passed on to their children, financial advisors are beginning to speak of the practice of "intergenerational planning."

Throughout this book, I seek the advice of those who have not just knowledge, but wisdom, about these sensitive subjects and what to do in these often trying circumstances. I hope you will get not only a general understanding of "how to," but also of "why to." For example, I'd like you to understand not just how the latest tax laws on inheritance work, but why it's important to seek the help of an attorney and to review your estate plan periodically.

This book does not purport to be a comprehensive work on estate planning or an exhaustive how-to on money management. Rather, I'd like to address the issues unique to inheritors in a manner that is both compassionate (I've been there, too) and objective (I'm not pushing a product or service). Although I am writing mainly for adults who receive an inheritance from their parents, much of the information applies as well to those who must deal with estates after the death of spouses, siblings, and others.

The book is intended to guide you through the stages of inheriting. The first chapters look at the "great expectations" created by the ongoing wealth transfer from the

World War II generation to their children and discuss how adult children and their parents can plan the transfer together while preserving family harmony. Middle chapters deal with both the "how to" aspects of inheritance as well as the emotional burdens that affect financial decisions. The final chapters examine your new role as inheritor, as you decide what legacy you plan to leave your own children, how you want to share what you have and how to know whether you're "heirworthy."

It wasn't until several years after my inheritance that I gradually adapted the estate to fit the needs of myself, my husband, and our two sons. The inheritance has helped us buy a larger house, save for retirement and college, and allowed me the flexibility to become self-employed, work from home, and spend more time with my sons.

Inherited money is *not* like other money. Don't squander it. Regard it as your "inheritance venture capital," a rare opportunity to enhance your life, in ways that you define.

For one of the first articles I wrote about inheritors, I remember asking Henry E. Zapisek, a financial planner who specializes in windfalls, whether inheritance made people's lives better. He responded, "An inheritance might or might not make your life more enjoyable, but it will almost certainly complicate it."

I hope, at the very least, that this book will help make your life less complicated, and at most, that it will help you find joy in your good fortune.

Chapter 1

The Great Wealth Transfer

Money is always there, pockets change.
—Gertrude Stein

How quickly the time went. We've gone from the Pepsi to the Probate Generation. Remember those television ads inviting us to join a carefree group of beautiful young people romping on the beach? Now we 76 million baby boomers are middle-aged and laden with responsibilities—jobs, mortgages, children, and aging parents. But we are still sought out by advertisers. They know we're coming into a lot of money, the largest transfer of wealth the world has ever seen.

Our "great expectations" were first quantified by two Cornell University researchers in 1993. Robert Avery and Michael Rendall estimated that the baby boomers would receive at least $10.4 trillion in inheritances from their parents between 1990 and 2040. This would account for 115 million bequests, according to the study, starting with 900,000 in 1990, rising to 2.8 million in 2005, peaking at 3.4 million in 2015, and then dropping off gradually until 2040. The annual amount of the bequests would start at $40 billion the first year, grow to $217 billion in 2005 and peak at $336 billion in 2015, before winding down in the other direction.[1]

As vast as these numbers are, they will likely turn out to be much larger. The prediction was made using 1989 dollars. Inflation, plus the tremendous run-up in the prices of homes and stocks in the 1990s, could double or even triple the size of the bequests.

A more recent study released in 1999 from Boston College that covers a longer period, includes a larger population, and takes into account the prosperity surge of the 1990s, forecasts a transfer between 1998 and 2055 of at least $41 trillion and as much as $136 trillion. This study by John Havens and Paul Schervish also includes the wealth passed from the boomers to their children.[2]

Any way you slice it, this intergenerational transfer of wealth is unprecedented. But what does it mean for our economy? And for the millions of inheritors?

It's helpful to think of this movement of assets not like an avalanche of wealth, but more like the slow and inexorable movement of a glacier. In any given year, says Avery, the money left through inheritance nationwide is not enough to fundamentally alter the economy or impact a recession. But for an individual, an inheritance can be life changing. Avery estimates that an inheritance managed wisely can boost an individual's wealth by 25 percent or more.

"There are a lot of people in the world counting on this money," says Olivia Mellan, a Washington, D.C., psychologist who specializes in money issues. These people view inheritance as freeing or transforming. Prospective inheritors shouldn't put their lives on hold while awaiting their bequests, however. While it's possible to make an educated guess about how much money an entire generation might bequeath, it is much more difficult to predict one family at a time. Members of the older generation, though they hold more than half the nation's wealth, are living longer and therefore spending more money than previous generations.

As families are discovering, the cost of medical care during the last few months of a loved one's life can easily consume an inheritance of several hundred thousand dollars. One woman who helped care for her late father recalls, "We were running through his money like water. Six more months and he would have been bankrupt." Instead, she says, "There will be a nice hunk of money to invest in my son's college fund. I never really expected that."

The Bequest Breakdown

Some baby boomers will get their inheritance in dribs and drabs, or not at all. In fact, many Americans will be left out of this transfer. A full one-third of all assets bequeathed, or $3.5 trillion, will go to the ultrarich, the top 1 percent of the nation's families, according to Avery and Rendall. A second third is destined for the top 10 percent of affluent Americans, and the remaining third will be parceled out among the other 90 percent of the population. Those who do receive an inheritance will get $90,000 on average (in 1989 dollars).

Clearly, the baby boomers are the beneficiaries of their parents' frugality. Reared in the Depression, tested by World War II, this "greatest generation" is also one of the greatest and most successful generation of savers. Even in their retirement years, many find it difficult to spend the money they have. "A lot of people who grew up in the Depression never planned to be wealthy and they don't think of what they have as wealth, even if it's $5 million," says Richard J. Muscio, a CPA and estate planner.

Their children, however, grew up with a different attitude toward money, forged during the sixties and seventies, when inflation was often a formidable force. Borrowing, rather than saving, was the way to accumulate assets. Because of inflation, the money you borrowed would cost you less in real dollars in future years, so it made sense to leverage the purchase of a home or business. Baby boomers also got hooked on consumer credit, however. While their parents are inclined to live below their means, baby boomers have no compunction about living beyond it.

So how will these new inheritors manage their windfalls? Economist Avery believes they will follow familiar patterns and simply consume them, rather than invest for the future. Although many heirs will be at least middle class if not affluent, they are not financially secure. As part of the "Sandwich Generation," balancing the needs of the generations before and after them, they face a financial triple-whammy, struggling to finance their children's education and to care for elderly parents while simultaneously trying to save for their own retirement. All too often, their own retirement savings are put off.

The Insecure Inheritor

But this is a risky approach, according to a 1997 research report by Phoenix Duff & Phelps entitled "The American Dream Reconsidered: The Hopes, Fears and Dreams of the American Affluent in the 1990s." The report says that while the affluent (those with income greater than $100,000 and net worth of more than $660,000) are at the top of their professions, their future prospects are uncertain. "Their work environment is haunted by downsizing, reengineering and phase-outs." They lack the job and retirement security their parents enjoyed.[3]

Many inheritors will be members of this growing affluent class, which has been called variously the upper middle class, the over-class, and the ultra middle class. But it would be wrong to think of them as heirs in the traditional sense, like a Rockefeller or a Kennedy. The affluent Americans interviewed for the report expected to receive on average an inheritance of $210,000, and one third of the group thought theirs would be less than $100,000.

"They are not the rich," states the Phoenix report. "The affluent depend on their jobs and careers to maintain their standard of living. Neither are the affluent the freewheelers and big spenders many think them to be; instead, they are hard-working families with traditional values." The message is clear: If they want to preserve their dreams for themselves and their children, they must continue to work hard—and to shepherd their inheritances wisely and well.

For even if they manage to keep their trigenerational families afloat financially, boomers could face a demographic backwash set off by their sheer numbers. The 76 million Americans born between 1946 and 1964 have strained every system they've encountered: sending school enrollments soaring in the 1950s and 1960s and prompting new school construction, flooding the job market in the 1970s and slowing wage growth, buying homes in the 1970s and contributing to soaring real estate prices, and, most recently, purchasing stocks through 401(k)s, thereby fueling the great bull market of the late 1990s.

So what happens when boomers go to cash out their investments to pay for their retirements? A study by Stanford University economist John Shoven and Wyatt Corp. economist Sylvester Schieber suggests that the massive sell-off of pension and retirement funds as baby boomers retire could depress investment values. "It doesn't seem too much of a stretch," says Shoven, "to think that something like the housing price run-up of the 1970s will be played out in reverse in the second and third decades of the twenty-first century, although this time the assets affected could be stocks, long-term bonds, houses and perhaps even gold."

Of course, no one can predict what will happen that far in the future. The authors say it's possible that boomers could offload their stocks to investors from developing countries like China and India as they enter our financial markets. But Shoven and Schieber warn not to expect a bailout. Instead, they say, the Big Chill generation can best keep themselves warm in retirement by saving and saving still more, while continuing to work past age sixty-five.

THE GREAT WEALTH transfer will accelerate the creation of a socioeconomic class I've dubbed the McMillionaires. During the 1990s, the number of households with net worth of more than $1 million more than doubled, from 2.6 million to more than 7 million, with the potential to grow to 20 million by 2010. The arrival of an inheritance of several hundred thousand dollars will help tip many affluent families over the $1 million net-worth mark.

McMillionaires, so common there will seem to be one on every corner, will by their very numbers devalue the idea of millionaire as economically independent. Indeed, this group will be prosperous but not truly wealthy, because they must work to maintain their lifestyles. And they will differ from "the millionaire next door" described in the best-selling book of the same name as an industrious male business owner and a stay-at-home wife who live below their means. The McMillies, by contrast, are dual-income hard-charging families living at or above their means, struggling to juggle their need to fund their retirement with the requirements of their children and aging parents.

How will Americans spend their inheritances? This is hard to say. But a 1998 survey undertaken for the financial products firm Lutheran Brotherhood offers a guide. Asked how they would spend a sizable windfall, the most popular choices were either a home (31 percent of those surveyed) or an education (30 percent). Ten percent chose a vacation, 9 percent picked a car, and 3 percent elected to help children or family members. Only 2 percent would pay off debt and a mere 1 percent would invest it. "People don't seem to have lavish dreams about what they would do right away with a larger inheritance or lottery prize," concluded a Lutheran Brotherhood spokesman. "Instead, Americans would just want a home to live in and an education to secure their futures."[4]

As they sell off their parents' homes and other assets, heirs will be left with cash to invest. It's likely that they will invest somewhat differently from their parents, due to the difference in age and generational temperament. For example, forty-five-year-old parents wanting to invest for their children's education will probably consider stock and bond mutual funds rather than the bank certificates of deposit on which so many seniors rely. The movement of funds from low-yielding deposits at bank institutions to higher-yielding investments in the general market is known as "disintermediation," a trend that investment management companies are awaiting with eagerness.

"A lot of the investment community is excited about this transfer of wealth," says Avery. That's because boomers are more likely than their parents to seek financial advice. So major institutions have surveyed these prospective inheritors, tailored ads to suit them, and offered to demystify the world of estates and planning. For example, Fidelity Investments, the nation's largest mutual fund company, created something it called Fidelity Legacy Services noting that "decisions customers make may affect more than one generation." Among the services the company offered were online educational materials and an estate planning calculator at its web site.

Inheritance Ambivalence

Americans have a love-hate relationship with inheritance. On the one hand, most of us would like to receive a bequest from our parents someday, just as property has been handed down from one generation to another for centuries. On the other hand, our nation is built upon the notion of individual opportunity, so that getting ahead, we like to believe, is based on merit and not on who your parents are and how much money they left you. Each year these two kinds of wealth seem to duke it out on the Forbes 400 list of wealthiest Americans. Vying for the top spot in recent years have been two self-made billionaires, Microsoft founder Bill Gates and renowned investor Warren Buffett. But at least seven of the top twenty spots are usually held down by heirs of those who created great fortunes, the Walton family of the Wal-Mart empire and the Mars family of the Mars candy dynasty.

As poet Ogden Nash so deftly put it: "Some people's money is merited/And other people's is inherited."

This ambivalence about inheritance runs through our history, starting with the founding fathers, according to Robert K. Miller, Jr., and Stephen J. McNamee, editors of the book *Inheritance of Wealth in America*. American leaders have long struggled to decide whether an inheritance is a natural right with which government shouldn't interfere or whether it should be subject to regulation, even to the point of reallocating the wealth of a person no longer living.

Thomas Jefferson and other revolutionaries argued for redistribution, fearing that letting the dead control property was a danger to the new nation, which they reasoned, belonged to the living. It's not surprising that the founding fathers would have harsh views on inheritance, given that they had defeated a monarchy whose wealth and power were passed from generation to generation regardless of merit.

A Taxing Debate

Eventually, inheritance rights in the new nation were subject to the power and taxation of government. But the merit versus inherit debate has never gone away. In the late 1800s, as the industrial revolution widened the gap between rich and poor, wealthy industrialist Andrew Carnegie joined with populists in an unsuccessful movement to curtail the power of rich family dynasties to pass wealth to future generations. A similar movement in 2001, led by billionaire investor Warren Buffett and the father of Bill Gates, tried unsuccessfully to preserve the estate tax as a means of encouraging meritocracy. Instead, Congress passed legislation that would phase out estate taxes in 2010 (only to have them reinstated in 2011 if no new legislation passes). See Chapter 13 for more on estate planning.

Despite the philosophical debates about inheritance, federal estate taxes have been imposed over the years for strictly practical reasons—to raise cash for war efforts.

They were first levied in 1797 in the undeclared naval war with France. The tax was repealed, then adopted, several times more to create a war chest. It was revived in 1916, during World War I, and has remained in effect ever since. It's probably no coincidence that in the decade before Congress agreed to reduce and eventually repeal the estate tax in 2010, the United States had not been involved in any long-term wars for twenty-five years—and that elected officials themselves stood to benefit from the great wealth transfer. If the war against terrorism proves both lengthy and costly, it is likely the estate tax will not be repealed after all.

Economists can't seem to agree on how big a role inheritance plays in helping individuals accumulate wealth. Researchers in the field refer to the "law of 20/80" because their best estimates suggest inheritance represents as little as 20 percent or as much as 80 percent of an inheritor's total wealth.

Whatever the size of your inheritance, it represents a great opportunity—to save for your retirement, to start a business, or to help your child through college. For spendthrift baby boomers, it can be a chance to grow up financially and start down a better path. After all, you might be thinking, what will I leave my heirs?

For a time in the late 1990s, news of the great windfalls received by dot.com investors and employees with high-tech stock options eclipsed that of the intergenerational wealth-transfer crowd. But the time-honored way of getting a financial boost is back: "I earned my money the old-fashioned way. I inherited it." Now comes your challenge. What will you make of it?

Chapter 2

Planning Together

If you want someone to water the flowers at your grave,
you've got to talk with them beforehand.
—Peg Eddy, financial planner

Talk to Your Parents

You know that your parents won't be with you for-ever. You should have "that talk" with them, but don't know where to begin. Is this, you wonder, payback for having to stumble through the dreaded facts-of-life talk with you when you were a teenager?

When it comes to estate planning, most Americans tend to practice a civilian version of "don't ask, don't tell." If you don't ask, they won't tell you. And if you do ask, they still might not tell you. Broaching the subject of your parents' finances and their estate plan can be touchy, no matter how open your family.

Although it was my eminently practical mother who first approached me with a list of her assets, I felt uncomfortable. She was in reasonably good health then, but I felt if I dwelled on the matter, it would make her think I was eager to get my hands on her money. And I didn't want to contemplate the eventuality of her death or somehow hasten it by planning for it. She also had me select an estate-planning attorney and accompany her to the appointments, so I could participate fully.

Picking Up After Dinner

But the experience I had with my husband's parents is more typical of how families share their estate plans—by bits and crumbs, often dropped after holiday meals. I was sitting with my in-laws in their kitchen after a Christmastime dinner, while my husband and two boys watched TV in the next room, when they began to ask me about estate planning. Because I wrote about personal finance, this didn't seem unusual. Before I knew it, they were talking about the size of their estate, at least $500,000, they told me with some pride. And they assured me they had a will and planned to divide their estate evenly between my husband and his brother. I commended them for having carried out an estate plan. It was a pleasant talk and they seemed pleased to share the information with me.

When I later told my husband and my brother-in-law about the discussion, they were incredulous: "What did they say?" they asked. I filled them in, and they admitted it was the first they'd heard of it. My husband confessed that he never would have initiated a talk because in his parents' eyes he would always be a kid. And parents simply didn't discuss such things with children.

Financial planner Peg Eddy has seen this situation many times. When it comes to discussing money with their adult children, she says, a parent might find it hard "to listen to the child who lost his lunch money every day." Once a kid, always a kid, it seems. One financial advisor told me that he had a 104-year-old client who still thought of her eighty-plus offspring as "the kids" and would parcel money out to them with care, saying, "I don't want the kids to have too much money."

In the years since, I've come to think of my in-laws' talk with me as no casual slip of the tongue, but rather a less awkward end run around having the emotionally charged talk. I think, in the end, that all four members of the immediate family were relieved that the message was delivered.

MANY PARENTS STILL adhere to the Northern European tradition of putting the eldest son in charge of managing the estate after their deaths, regardless of his qualifications or interest in being executor. Of course, the job might be handled more capably by a daughter or a younger son, as in the following example.

Richard J. Muscio, a CPA and estate planner, says his father casually mentioned that he had named Muscio's older brother as trustee of their parents' trust. Muscio was taken aback because helping trustees manage estates was how he made his living. When Muscio's father told the brother of his decision, the brother nearly fell out of his chair. You're the oldest son, his father explained. "But I'd just have to hire Dick to do it all," the brother replied. So the father named Muscio as trustee, to the relief of both brothers.

If you don't have a clue about your parents' estate, you're not alone. "Most parents don't sit down with their kids and say, 'Here's what my will says,' " says economist Robert Avery. "It's socially taboo. That makes it a big mystery." Many older Americans are part of a generation that believes finances are private matters and has no concept of "financial parenting."

While nearly three-fourths of adults say it's easy to talk about inheritance matters with their family, according to a survey by Fidelity Investments, 41 percent of adults who have already received an inheritance of more than $50,000 say they never spoke about the bequests with those who left it to them, usually a parent.

An Emotional Landmine

Approaching your parents about their finances and their estate can make them feel old, incapable of managing their own affairs. Money management is often one of the last tasks seniors will relinquish to others when they're in failing health. They might worry that you're only concerned about getting the inheritance. Grown children might be reluctant to start the conversation for the same reason. "They don't want to appear to be vultures in the tree waiting for them to die," says Muscio. And if a parent has remarried after divorce or windowhood, he or she might want to avoid the inevitable conflict in divvying up an inheritance between the children from a previous marriage and the new spouse. The result is often procrastination.

Some parents don't want to discuss inheritance, because they fear their children will have no self-motivation if they learn they will be getting a substantial bequest. Others are concerned about outliving their money, and don't want to make promises that can't be kept.

Adult children have their own highly charged reasons for avoiding the subject. "Nobody wants to give up being a kid," says Susan Richards, a Chicago certified financial planner. "You're taking a step down a path where the nature of your relationship is going to change." And both children and parents often dread the discussion because it is really about disability and death.

SUSAN RICHARDS IS the author of a book called *Protect Your Parents and Their Financial Health . . . Talk with Them Before It's Too Late.* She was motivated to write her book after her own failed attempt to talk to her late father, who had been a successful businessman. Richards knew it was important that she learn about her widowed father's financial affairs, and she handed him a list of questions she wanted answered. He stopped her in her tracks and said, "Everything is taken care of."

However, he suffered a severe stroke six months later. Initially, Richards found herself struggling to make important decisions. She was forced to make vital health-care choices without knowing what kind of supplemental insurance her father had, to take care of his car (damaged as a result of the stroke) without knowing the name of his insurer, and to pay his bills without knowing where to locate his checkbook. "If you don't know where things are," says Richards, "it's just a tremendous hardship."

Talking to our parents about their possible disabilities and inevitable deaths can be difficult and painful. And we dread both knowing and not knowing about any inheritance (How much will I get? Will I get less than my siblings? Worse yet, what if there isn't any? What if I should be helping them?). Many of us would sooner launch ourselves in a rocket over the Grand Canyon Evel Knievel–style than introduce these topics to our parents. But if you don't want to spend the rest of your life regretting that you had unfinished business with your parents, you need to talk with them now. In my interviews with dozens of heirs, attorneys, financial advisors, and psychologists, I often heard sad tales that could have been avoided with some simple, straightforward conversation.

SOME PEOPLE UNDERSTAND intuitively how to leave their heirs well prepared. The mother of a woman named Sara, a Virginia editor, was one of them. Before she died of cancer, she gave away valuable and sentimental items to her three daughters. "We all got something meaningful and important," recalls Sara. Her mother also made it clear, to her daughters' relief, that she wanted a plain, simple casket. In addition to a will, the mother left a list of assets. "If a parent's able to do that," says Sara, "it's such a gift to the children."

Estate planners say that the biggest problems in settling estates occur when inheritors are treated unequally or had expectations that were unrealistic and couldn't be met. Most siblings expect to be treated equally. Says Muscio:

"If you're not going to treat the kids equally, all the more reason to tell them." Parents need not go into great detail or disclose the amounts, but they can describe how they're going to distribute what they have.

When people make an estate plan, they tend to think of it as a distasteful chore to be completed quickly. They might give little thought to what it feels like to be on the receiving end. For the beneficiaries, what is laid out there can seem like the final chapter in an all-important relationship, a judgment, a stamp of approval, or a vote of no confidence. Your parents might not realize the consequences of what they're planning—unless you begin talking to them.

Equality and Harmony

Many estate planning experts believe parents should divide their estate fairly—if not equally—whenever possible among all their children. Unequal giving can have unintended consequences. For example, a parent might decide to disinherit a wayward son and leave it all to the dutiful daughter. This should make the daughter happy, right? Not exactly. The brother will probably assume the sister colluded with the parent and take out his bitterness on her. Now her parent is dead and she's estranged from her nearest living relative over something she didn't do.

Nor is it necessarily appropriate for parents to leave their daughter, the high-tech mogul, or their son, the wealthy developer, out of the estate because they don't "need" the money. To assume they wouldn't mind is to misjudge human nature. True, they might not need the money, and might even give it to a needier sibling or to charity, but they don't want to be disinherited by their parents.

A friend of mine has two sisters, one who married a wealthy man and one who had never been able to hold a job long and had a history of money problems. Her widowed mother was thinking of cutting the married sister out of the $6 million estate and giving her share to the needy sister. My friend implored her mother not to do that to her sister. "Even if she doesn't need it, it wouldn't feel good for her," my friend told her mother. "And we have no idea what will happen to her life in the future." Finally, the mother agreed. My friend had the foresight to consider how individual family members would feel after her mother's death and she didn't want them to feel alienated from one another.

Disparate gifts from parents to children can be a problem before a parent's death, as well after. Did your brother get his tuition and all expenses to private medical school paid while you worked your way through state college? Or perhaps you're the one who received $50,000 seed money to start a new business, while your two siblings went to work for large companies straight out of school. Was that money a loan or a gift? You might not be keeping score, but your siblings most likely are. These differences in parental largesse are common and don't necessarily cause problems. But sometimes resentments over these gifts now can develop into full-blown feuds over the inheritance later. If such inequalities are a sore subject, try to persuade your parents to talk about them now while there is time. Believe it or not, children ask their parents to address this—and parents (who might not recognize their behavior until it's pointed out to them) do sometimes balance the accounts. If the parents don't have the money now, they might rectify the situation in their estate plans. Or the parents might simply talk to all the siblings together and simply acknowledge that they can't make up for financial inequity, which might go a long way toward healing any wounds.

Better to Know Now

Heirs should know if they're getting more or less than they expected. Your sister needs to know that she's not getting the family china and your spendthrift brother must be told that his share will be held for him in trust. It's not that your parents owe you an inheritance. They don't. But benefactors show true generosity and courage when they explain their decisions to their heirs. Olivia Mellan, a Washington psychologist and author, advocates sorting problems out before the transfer is made. Rather than deal with the child who's got a spending problem by leaving money in trust, says Mellan, "It would be better to have this fight while the parent is still alive." That way, the child could at least attempt to change. Otherwise, after the parent dies, the child is frozen indefinitely in the role of irresponsible spender.

Many attorneys still advocate that parents keep silent on their estate plans. One to whom I spoke, James Lauth, says this approach provides maximum flexibility. If the parents want to change their plans, they can without stirring up hard feelings. A son who was initially disinherited can be brought back into the fold, none the wiser—and vice versa. And should parents fall on hard times or deplete their estates, the heirs are not fixated on what might have been.

Some inheritors believe, however, that keeping an inheritance close to the vest can be harmful even if the bequest turns out to be much more, rather than less, than beneficiaries expected. "Parents are famous for keeping secrets," says Valerie Jacobs, a steward to part of a family fortune and a psychologist who consults on inheritance and wealth issues. "It's just the worst thing you can do." The first reaction of inheritors to getting large sums of money after being kept in the dark is not joy, says Jacobs. It's anger at the notion that they couldn't handle the news earlier and regret that they had no chance to prepare for a major life change. And if they had questions about what to do with the largesse after the parents' deaths, says Jacobs, "It's a done deal. If they want any information, it's too late."

How to Get Started

Is there any way to begin a dialogue with your parents? Yes. Because the lack of communication between the generations on this subject is so pervasive and because so much money is about to be transferred, financial advisors have begun compiling some helpful approaches:

- Often the best means of opening communication is for you to get your own financial house in order first. That would include doing estate planning, having the necessary documents in place for emergencies, and compiling an inventory of assets and a document locator.

  Then you can matter-of-factly describe for Mom and Dad the value of such planning and ask if they themselves have given any thought to it. That way, you aren't asking your parents to do something you haven't done yourself. It gives you leverage. Also, this will allow you to gain an understanding of estate law so you can help answer your parents' questions or point out aspects of their situation that require attention.

  In fact, this very strategy might have set off the kitchen conversation with my in-laws. I had told them, after my mother died, that Tony and I, after much procrastinating, had finally done our estate planning. And what a relief it was to finish! That, in turn, might have given them a little impetus and made them more willing to talk with me.

- Consider your parents' financial history. If they've lived through the Depression or other hard times, they might regard your ability to handle money with suspicion. By comparison, you've known nothing but good times.

  On the other hand, your parents might be overwhelmed by the complexity of the modern world and would welcome your help. After all, they were reared in a simpler era, while you came of age amid an out-pouring of financial information and products, from *Money* magazine to junk bonds. If you are more adept at handling money matters, your best approach might go something like this: "You've done so much for me. I really want to be able to help you."

- Look for an appropriate time. If a friend of the family dies and the widow is having a hard time managing her finances, you could ask your parents if their estate plans are in order. The eve of a major trip or a surgery could provide an opening to inquire if there are any financial or legal matters that need to be addressed. "Plant the seed and then continue to water it," says Eddy. "Don't expect them to change overnight." Keep in mind, too, that you might be able to influence their behavior only up to a point.

- Share relevant articles from magazines and newspapers. Or better yet, get a subscription to a financial magazine that often deals with estate planning. Watch a television show on the subject together, any nonthreatening way to get the conversation started.

- Draft your siblings. When you approach your parents, you don't want to look as if you're trying to cut a side deal. So include all your siblings if possible. That will also help your message carry more weight.

- Suggest a financial "checkup." Rather than confront the estate planning issue directly, encourage your parents to see a financial advisor. Any good advisor will quickly recommend estate planning, if none has been done, or a review of existing documents. Coming from an authority outside of the family, the advice could be taken more seriously.

One caveat, however. If your parents go to visit your financial advisor or estate planning attorney, there is a built-in conflict of interest. Will the advice to your parents be skewed to benefit you, because you want to inherit from them? Your parents shouldn't accept the advisor on trust, but should do their own due diligence on the advisor's background and experience. And if they choose your advisor, they might have to sign a document acknowledging the potential conflict of interest.

- Be persistent. Some estate planning issues seem insoluble. How can your parents divide their estate equitably if most of it is tied up in the business, and you're the only one of the three children who works there? Or if your sister has taken care of your parents for the past ten years while you lived across the country? These difficult situations can result in avoidance. But your parents' problem is not unique. Good estate planning professionals encounter these issues frequently and can suggest a variety of options. Just remember that with complicated situations, sometimes there are no perfect answers.

- Try the businesslike approach. If all else fails, go straight to the bottom line. Look, Mom and Dad, if you don't do proper estate planning, the IRS will get $100,000 of your estate instead of your family or your favorite charity. Is that what you want? If you leave your estate in a mess, you will also burden your loved ones unnecessarily.

ADULT CHILDREN OFTEN wait until there's a crisis to begin asking about their parents' finances. But the best time to start is when they're feeling healthy and alert. Begin with the least invasive kinds of issues such as bill paying and health insurance before tackling more sensitive subjects like annual income and estate planning. Here's what adult children should try to learn from their parents:

- What kind of medical insurance do you have?
- Who are your doctors?
- What medications do you take?
- What are your monthly expenses?
- Where do you keep your financial records?
- How would I pay your routine bills, if I had to?
- Have you done any estate planning?
- Where are your estate planning documents?

For more information on how to plan an estate, see Chapter 13, Planning Your Own Estate.

Don't Overlook Personal Possessions

Some of the things we inherit have little monetary but great emotional value. You shouldn't feel embarrassed to ask a parent about a small or sentimental item you would treasure—especially if it's one that could easily get tossed into a Goodwill bag when you aren't around. My husband asked his mother for his father's thick, old-fashioned baseball gloves. A friend of mine, whose father fished for a living, wanted the gearshift knob from his tuna boat. One Southern California couple in their sixties told me they were surprised when all three of their children asked to have the same personal item: a large, framed manuscript of words to live by, written by their grandfather, entitled, "Guides to My Grandchildren." Each grandchild already had a nicely framed copy, but wanted the original. So they drew straws.

"Personal possessions are a big, big issue," says attorney Shirley Kovar, an attorney who practices in the growing field of estate mediation. She frequently sees pitched battles over personal effects, like books, china, jewelry, doll collections, cars, or sentimental items of almost no value, such as a $35 Boogie Board. The strangest dispute of all, however, was a family feud over a Christmas ornament. Stranger still, the family was Jewish. Objects give continuity to our lives and help us connect to other generations.

If there are going to be hard feelings over mom's wedding ring, dad's golf clubs, or the refurbished '56 Chevy, sort out the problem now and you could reach a compromise. If your parents put it off until it's too late, however, they might have set off a time bomb. There's a reason that inheritors often want the same personal items, such as mom's silver or dad's tools, says Nancy A. Spector, estate planning attorney. It's not for their monetary value, but for what they represent—namely who will carry on the family name and tradition.

Some older people actually seem to enjoy deciding who will get which piece of personal property. One attorney told me of a client who pasted sticky dots—color-coded by heir—on the bottom of each of his household items. A woman in her nineties had painstakingly taped the names of her heirs to pieces of furniture and name-tagged mountains of quilts with safety pins.

And, of course, some parents enjoy giving away some of their estates before they die—in the form of a down payment for a house, college education for the grandkids, or a simple keepsake. Some heirs regard this as a blessing, while others find it a distasteful reminder of their parents' mortality. But unless your parents can't afford the bequest or unless it comes with burdensome strings attached, I wouldn't discourage your parents from giving part of their estate away during their lives. My friend Catherine treasures the memory of her ailing father pulling a Ziploc bag from a drawer filled with her late mother's costume jewelry. Catherine herself didn't much care for the jewelry. But she says, "I just can't get rid of it, remembering the pleasure of my dad when he gave it to me."

YOU'D LIKE TO gather your siblings together to talk to your parents about who will inherit dad's tools and mom's china, but you fear out-and-out warfare. Not to worry. There's guidance for passing on personal possessions available from an excellent step-by-step workbook called *Who Gets Grandma's Yellow Pie Plate?* ($12.50) created by the University of Minnesota Extension Service. As the introduction notes, "There can be powerful messages in who gets what. Planning ahead allows for more choices, the opportunity for communication, and fewer misunderstandings and conflicts." The workbook walks users through six steps including what is to be accomplished with the transfer, deciding what is "fair" in the context of each family, and managing conflicts. To order write Minnesota Extension Service Distribution Center, 20 Coffey Hall, 1420 Eckles Avenue, St. Paul, MN. 55108-6068, e-mail *order@extension.umn.edu* or call 800-876-8636.

Life's Inventory

Many people assume they're done with estate planning once they've signed the wills or dotted all the *i*'s on their trusts. It's a good idea, however, and a great act of consideration to go one step further: to take inventory.

Consider this: Do you know how many life insurance policies your parents have? Or where they are? Do you know where they keep their valuables? In a safe deposit box, a home safe, a hiding place, or all three? Do you know the value and location of all of their assets?

Here's why you should. An accountant once worked with two daughters who inherited hundreds of thousands of baseball cards from their father. The women hadn't a clue that dad's hobby had any worth and they were planning to give the cards away. Fortunately, the accountant intervened, and the collection was appraised at $80,000. Another family of grown children stumbled upon $20,000 worth of government bonds two years after their mother died—thrown in with boxes of worthless papers in her garage.

It's not uncommon for those who grew up during the Depression to keep cash, coins, or jewels hidden in the house. Ralph Warner learned this to his amazement one day when his mother casually mentioned that she kept

$20,000 in jewelry and cash at the base of a lamp. Not just any lamp, but one he considered extremely ugly and would have put out on the street for a Salvation Army truck to pick up in an instant. Warner is cofounder of Nolo Press and coauthor of Nolo's *Personal RecordKeeper* software program. That incident prompted him to include a category in his software called "Hiding Places."

Warner's is one of a dozen software programs and books designed to help families get their affairs in order and make life simpler for their beneficiaries. "Don't put your heirs through hell while you're in heaven" is the motto of Martin Kuritz, coauthor of a fill-in, notebook style organizer called *The Beneficiary Book*. Such books and programs can be a great help because they provide prompting lists and suggestions: not just where are the bank accounts and investments, but who grooms the dog, repairs the car, and cleans the swimming pool. They also provide space for family history, medical histories, and personal remembrances.

Of course, anyone can take inventory with just a pen and paper. Here are the essential items to include:

- All checking and savings accounts, brokerage accounts and mutual funds, with account numbers and locations.
- All life insurance and medical policies.
- Individual stocks owned, the number of shares, and where they are held.
- Retirement accounts, such as company pensions, 401(k)s, IRAs, or Keoghs.
- Location of all safe-deposit boxes, an inventory of the contents, and where to find the keys.

- All assets of value. Go from room to room and don't skip the garage.
- Location of hidden assets.
- A list of all collections and their value.

Use a computer program if possible and update regularly.

Finally, have your parents give a copy of their personal inventory to a trusted person outside their home, such as an executor or advisor. These lists are also invaluable in the event of disasters, floods, earthquakes, and fires for documenting insurance losses.

ARE YOU THE "AIR" APPARENT?

AMERICANS HOLD MORE than $40 billion worth of frequent flier miles, but often don't think to specify a beneficiary for them in their estate plans. Thus, these airlines rewards are increasingly the subject of family disputes, says Randy Petersen, publisher of *Insider Flyer* and frequent flyer mileage expert witness. He testified in one case that pitted the adult granddaughter of a doting, well-traveled grandfather against his widow. The young woman felt she should get the hundreds of thousands of miles, because her grandfather routinely bestowed the freebies on her. But the widow thought she was entitled to them as a source of consolation and a ticket to world travel in her final years. The judge sided with the granddaughter, citing grandpa's apparent plans to continue giving them to her.

If your parents are high fliers, how can they be sure their free miles go to the right inheritor? Attorney James Miller says

they should ask each airline for guidance on naming beneficiaries, then add a specific provision in their wills, especially if
the recipients are not the primary benefactors. Then they
should be certain to tell their "air" apparents of their plans.

Even if you never persuade your parents to plan their
estates, you must succeed in getting them to sign two
critical documents in the event of their incapacity, for
their sake as well as yours. One document names who
would be responsible for managing their finances and the
other names who would be responsible for making decisions about their health, should they became incapacitated. I can't stress enough how important these legal
documents are. They can save you and your parents hours
of anxiety, heartbreak, frustration, and possible court in-
volvement. One inheritor who cared for his father
through months of illness before his death said he
couldn't imagine trying to cope without the two powers
of attorney: "They were just so necessary."

Point out to your parents that anyone (including you)
can become incapacitated at any time. A forty-year-old in
a coma following a traffic accident needs these just as
much as an eighty-year-old who's suffered a stroke. These
documents do not imply that they are getting senile or
can't manage their own affairs. In fact the earlier people
execute them the better, because they must be mentally
competent when signing.

Many people just assume that if they became too ill to
manage their personal finances, a family member could
easily walk in and take over. You might think, "Well, I'm

the daughter. I'm going to step in." But not even a spouse or grown child can negotiate Social Security payments, deal with an IRA or annuity, file a tax return, open a safe deposit box, or sell a piece of property on behalf of the incapacitated person. Without the proper document, for example, in a case where a married couple own their home in joint tenancy and one develops Alzheimer's, the other spouse would be unable to sell the property to pay for care without getting a court's permission.

What happens when no legal precautions have been taken? You and your family could be headed for court, where a judge would appoint a conservator to manage your parent's financial affairs, and if necessary, a conservator or guardian would also be appointed to manage his or her health care. The court typically appoints a family member, friend, or a professional fiduciary. Legal experts say it's a procedure that's best avoided because the hearings can be costly, tedious, and even humiliating. The incapacitated person must be brought in or wheeled to court (unless deemed too ill to appear) so the judge can determine if a conservatorship is warranted. "It is emotionally very draining and demeaning to everyone," says Evelyne Hutkin, a gerontologist who serves as an advocate for the elderly in Southern California.

If a conservator of the estate is appointed, all assets must be inventoried. The conservator must also account for how all monies are spent. "The paperwork involved in a conservatorship is mind-boggling," says Spector.

Fortunately, there are commonly available legal documents that make conservatorship unnecessary. These don't have to be prepared at an attorney's office, but it's a good idea to have an attorney review them.

- Durable power of attorney for financial matters. With this document, you can give broad powers to another, trusted person to manage your financial affairs. Your "agent" can take many actions depending on how the document is worded: pay bills, sign for Social Security benefits, make investments, and even prepare your estate plan. It is important that the power be "durable." That means it remains effective indefinitely, even when you are incapacitated, presumably when you need it the most.

  But some people aren't comfortable giving another person wide latitude with their finances. Instead, they can opt for a document called a "springing power of attorney," meaning the power is effective only upon their disability—as they define it in the document.

  It's best to have the power of attorney signed while the person is clearly competent, advises attorney Ellen L. van Hoften. If it's a close case, where the person has good days and bad days, have two witnesses document that the person was competent when signing the power of attorney.

  A statutory form for powers of attorney can be purchased at stationery shops. Generally, such documents must be either notarized or witnessed by two persons.

Another way of having a backup manager for your finances is to use this popular estate planning tool:

- A living trust. This legal device allows you to keep full control over property in the trust while you are alive, and quickly transfers trust property to your beneficiaries upon your death, avoiding the cost and hassle of probate. Trusts are commonly touted to avoid probate, the legal process of administering an estate through a court, but they can also avoid conservatorship.

Typically, the person who sets up the trust transfers his or her assets into it and then manages them as the trustee. The trust document names a successor trustee (typically a spouse, family member, private fiduciary, or trust company) to assume control should the original trustee die or become incapacitated. The trust can contain specific wording that sets the standard for determining the trustee's incompetence—whether, for example, the declarations of one or two physicians are required.

The downside of living trusts is that they must be funded—that is, that ownership of all appropriate assets such as real estate, investments, and bank accounts must be transferred to the trust. Vigilantly keeping the assets in the trust can be a chore over time. Buying a new home or refinancing an existing one, for example, can trigger the need to title property in the name of the trust. Spector cites the case of a seventy-five-year-old woman who suffered a stroke. She had a living trust and had placed her home in it, but not $350,000 in investments. Thus, it was necessary for her nephew to be named her conservator so he could manage her money. "Don't leave property outside the trust," says Spector.

"The successor trustee has no authority over assets not in the trust."

Because of the possibility of such oversights, attorneys recommend that anyone with a living trust also sign a power of attorney for finances. That way, too, the agent can oversee assets that shouldn't be placed in the trust, such as IRAs, pension plans, stock options, annuities, and insurance.

The inability to manage financial affairs is usually brought on by ill health. That's why all of us need the next document.

- Durable power of attorney for health care. This document, also called a health-care proxy, gives another person the power to make medical decisions for you when you're not able. Hutkin, the gerontologist, says she frequently finds that older people have named someone to handle their finances but not their health. "I find it most frustrating that we all value our money much more than we value our body," she says. Most people avoid signing this document, she says, "because it's a very scary thing to be thinking of." Yet, without it, even an individual who has a living trust and a durable power of attorney for financial matters could end up in a conservatorship. A properly executed and notarized power of attorney for health care should make a conservatorship of the person unnecessary.

  If you feel strongly about having your wishes followed should you become seriously ill, make certain that you also prepare a "declaration," also known as a "living will." The declaration is a written statement to your doctors detailing what kind of care you would and would not want. In most states, you can indicate whether you want all, some, or no life-prolonging procedures followed. Some states combine the two documents, the declaration and the durable power of attorney for health care, into one.

Many people, unfortunately, view signing a power of attorney as giving up control. But it's really just the opposite, say attorneys and financial experts. "Without a power of attorney," says Richards, "they've given up total control." The key, of course, is giving the powers of attorney only to individuals who are highly trust-worthy.

LET'S SAY YOUR widowed mother has all her financial and estate planning affairs in order. But there's only one problem. You live in Connecticut and she lives in Des Moines. As she gets older and more forgetful, you wonder how well she's managing. You can't clone yourself to go live with her. Who will watch over her?

A growing number of families are turning to private fiduciaries. A fiduciary is a person or an institution that manages finances and other personal affairs on behalf of others. Once, their services were offered through banks to the very wealthy, but now many work independently and assist the middle class as well as the rich. Some offer a wide variety of personal services—such as hiring home-care providers, helping with nursing home placement, and even making sure that pets are vaccinated and licensed. Private fiduciaries are responding to changes in society, such as the increasing longevity of the population and the tendency of grown children to live far from elderly parents, says Spector. "There's a real need for them," she says. "It's the same kind of thing as day care. Who needed day care fifty years ago? The world has changed."

Maureen Neumayer, an officer of the Professional Fiduciary Association, says her goal is often to help keep elderly clients in their own homes. One vulnerable lady was receiving as many as thirty contest solicitations in the mail per day until Neumayer put a stop to it. An elderly man was so convinced he was going to win a new-car contest that she had to persuade him not to hire contractors to build a garage for it.

The fees charged by a fiduciary can vary, though 1 percent of assets under management (such as the value of the person's house and investments) per year is common. Special services, such as selling a business or a house, can add to the cost. For more on hiring fiduciaries see Chapter 11, Getting Professional Help.

None of us likes to think about becoming too old or infirm to manage our own affairs. But in a time of crisis, health-care and financial management directives often prove invaluable. My mother had signed both a power of attorney for finances and one for health care before she became terminally ill. And when she could no longer manage for herself, I was thankful day in and day out for many weeks that I could rely on those documents.

I also used the power of attorney for health care numerous times, usually at the hospital working with doctors and nurses to chart her final days. The document gave me the power to speak for her, to follow through on her wishes, again without having to subject her to painful discussions of the obvious.

With the power of attorney for finances, I was able to pay her bills, file her income taxes, and make some last-minute changes in her estate plan before she died. With the presentation of that piece of paper, I could sign almost anything on her behalf without having to worry her about the particulars. She knew that I had simply stepped into her place.

Chapter 3

Delicate Circumstances

*You never know how truly complicated life can be until
you marry, have children, divorce, and remarry—and
accumulate enough wealth to start worrying about where
all the money will go that you can't take with you.
That's when you suddenly develop an interest
in estate planning.*
—Business Week, May 2, 1994

Estate planning can be especially difficult in either of
two commonplace situations: if your parents have
divorced and remarried, or if your parents' estate is
made up primarily of a family-owned business.

About half of all marriages in this country end in divorce. Some 40 percent of marital unions involve one
spouse who has been married before. In fact, we're well
on our way to having more stepfamilies than traditional
ones. And because of increased longevity, our parents often choose to remarry if they have been widowed.

As a result of all of the above, many baby boomers now
find themselves part of a parent's "blended family," where
raising the issue of inheritance can be a touchy subject.
No doubt Dad wants to provide for his new wife, but also
to leave something for his grown children. What Dad

might not realize is that spouses have certain property rights that other family members don't. Depending on the state of residence, a surviving spouse is automatically entitled to as much as half the estate of a spouse who dies without creating a will after the remarriage. Spouses also get priority when it comes to retirement plans. By doing nothing upon his remarriage, Dad could inadvertently disinherit his children and set his survivors up for years of turmoil. Without proper planning, here's the kind of confrontation that can unfold:

- Your mother leaves her entire estate to her second husband, who promises that upon his death he'll bequeath it to you and your siblings from her first marriage. She dies first. Then despite your pleas, your stepfather gives it all to his children. Or perhaps he remarries and decides to leave the estate to his new wife. "People make promises to each other, and they may well mean them at the time," says attorney Nancy A. Spector. No matter how much someone trusts a spouse, she says, the only way to ensure a bequest will go to the intended recipients is to put it in an estate plan. She's seen children distraught because their stepparent's relatives are eating off the heirloom china. "I hear nightmare stories about this all the time."

- Your dad puts some of his estate in trust for you and your two sisters, with income from the trust to benefit his second wife during her life. When she dies, the assets are to go to the three of you. This scenario can create a long waiting period in which you, your siblings, and the widow battle over how the trust is invested and how much she's taking out of it.

You three worry that she's draining all the assets, while she feels that you're monitoring her every move. The waiting can be greatly prolonged if your father remarried a younger woman. The widow could have many years of living ahead of her, while you wait decades to receive your inheritances.

- Your mother is a successful businesswoman who, after divorcing your father, remarries. She drafts a will leaving half her estate to her new husband and half to you and your brother. But when she dies, your stepfather gets most of the estate because he was named the beneficiary on her sizable Individual Retirement Account. An IRA or 401(k) account might hold most of the money contained in a person's estate, but it is unaffected by that person's will or trust. The money must go to the beneficiary or beneficiaries named on the account.

Disinheritance Dialogue

Richard J. Muscio, a CPA and estate planner, says that a parent's remarriage often leaves children feeling their money is being given to someone else. "The biggest messes we've seen are with more than one marriage and more than one set of kids," he says. "The key is communicating and managing expectations." Spector says it is essential in these situations to plan ahead. Have your parents walk through what would happen if the husband dies first or if the wife dies first. Then they should consult an estate planning attorney on how to carry out their wishes.

But communicating on these matters can be exceptionally tricky. Your parent and stepparent could be nervous about discussing it with each other, uncomfortable saying how much they want to leave each other or their respective children. You might feel able to discuss the issue with Mom, for example, but draw the line at talking with your stepdad. Nevertheless it's important to lay out what might happen and even to tell your parent, "I could be disinherited. Is that what you want?"

There are a number of tools for dealing with these issues, though no single one may be perfect. Some situations could require several approaches. In most cases, one spouse brings more assets to the marriage than the other, which can create inequities. It might not be possible to be generous with everyone. Here then are some of the methods:

- Gifting. Begin giving away part of the estate now. Anyone can give up to $11,000 away free of gift tax per year to anyone else. That means that your parent could give you $11,000 a year (or $22,000 if the stepparent cooperates) and a like amount to any grandchild each year tax free. Of course, your parents could give away even larger amounts (if they can afford it), but anyone who gives away more than $11,000 annually to any one person will be reducing their personal estate/gift tax exemption—that is, how much they'll be able to leave free of federal estate taxes upon their

deaths. The exemption is scheduled to increase gradually from $1 million in 2003 to $3.5 million in 2009,
with the estate tax to be repealed in 2010. However,
the repeal will last only one year, unless Congress acts.
- Pay-on-death (POD) accounts. If your mom wants a
  simple way to leave cash to you and your siblings after
  her death, she can set up POD accounts at a bank, also
  known as bank trust accounts, Totten trusts, or infor-
  mal trusts. She names a beneficiary for each account,
  but she controls the money and can withdraw it at any
  time. Unlike a joint account, it cannot be seized by
  your or your sibling's debtors. Though it will pass directly to you upon your mother's death without probate, it is still part of her estate.

  She could also hold Treasury securities and stocks
  and bonds in pay-on-death accounts. In most states,
  she can own stocks and bonds in brokerage accounts
  that transfer upon death to her beneficiaries. Again,
  such accounts bypass probate, but are included in her
  estate.
- Life insurance. This approach can be used by middle-
  class as well as affluent families to provide cash upon
  death to their children. Other assets can be left to the
  surviving spouse. For example, your fifty-year-old father could purchase a $200,000 term life insurance pol-
  icy on himself, naming you, the child from his first
  marriage, as beneficiary, for as little as $450 a year for
  ten years. The balance of his estate, say $200,000,
  could then go to his widow. Financial planners report
  increasing and successful usage of this method.

Anyone with an estate of more than $1 million (the 2003 threshold exemption for estate taxes, or $1.5 million in 2004–2005) who wants to leave more than that amount to heirs using life insurance can employ an irrevocable life insurance trust. If properly structured, funds from the trust would be free from estate taxes. To qualify, the insured person cannot own the policy. It must be held in an irrevocable trust, that is, one that once created can't be changed or terminated. In addition, the life insurance policy ideally should be a new one. Using a policy that existed prior to the trust (in cases where the insured can't readily obtain new insurance) is a risk. In such a case, if the insured person dies within three years of setting up the irrevocable trust, the insurance proceeds go back into the *taxable* estate.

- Trusts. These are commonly used by stepfamilies who want the same money to do two different jobs. Your father could put some or all of his assets in trust for you and your brothers, but allow his third and surviving wife to live off the trust income until she passes away. Only then are the assets distributed to you and your siblings. This approach might seem eminently fair, but it has pitfalls. Often the widow wants the assets managed to produce income, while you and your siblings want the assets to grow. If either the widow or you are in charge of managing the money, there is a conflict of interest. A trust company or private fiduciary should manage the trust instead. And even if a trusted family friend serves as the trustee, there should be a backup trustee—preferably not the children of either spouse—and a method for selecting a new trustee.

However, postponing your inheritance in this way can cause hard feelings. Spector recommends that parents using such a trust consider giving some money or property from the estate immediately upon their deaths to their children and grandchildren. "That keeps a lot of peace in the family," she says.

THE MAY-DECEMBER PROBLEM

IMAGINE THAT YOU'RE the favorite niece of your rich Uncle Harry, who built a fortune buying stocks cheap during the Depression. He married a second wife who was much younger, but you're his closest blood relative. When Uncle Harry died in 1965 he left you a cool $5 million. There's only one problem. He left the money in one of several trusts that can't be disbursed until his widow dies.

This story was told to me by Uncle Harry's great niece, Diane, the daughter of the $5 million heiress. As it turned out, Harry's widow lived a long time and outlasted his niece. Though the niece waited years for the money, all she received was $100,000 as her health was failing, according to Diane. "It was totally not what we had planned," says Diane. "The bitterness was there." When Uncle Harry's widow did pass away, thirty-five years after her husband, Diane received her mother's inheritance. It had shrunk to $800,000. The sad part was that Uncle Harry was wealthy enough to give money away immediately to his relatives and to keep his widow in comfort.

It's common in stepfamilies for the parent who owns the marital home to leave it to his or her children, but with the provision that the surviving spouse be allowed to live there during his or her lifetime. This can be accomplished through what is known as a marital property control trust. The trust should make clear who will pay for upkeep of the house, who owns which furniture, and what happens if the survivor remarries or stops living there on a regular basis. Again, this might seem like a fair compromise, but it could set up years of tense exchanges between a stepparent who needs a place to live and grown children who feel an emotional attachment to their family home.

- Separate property. Either by prenuptial agreement or less formal arrangement, a couple can keep their assets separate. This can be the cleanest way to do things in remarriages, especially among older spouses with adequate resources. A prenuptial agreement would describe which assets each spouse is keeping as separate property and which would be held jointly.
- Not marrying. This can be an option for older couples who want to retain their first spouse's benefits and also want to keep property separate for their children. Because of the significant financial ramifications, anyone with children from a previous relationship should carefully weigh the consequences of remarriage before taking this big step.

Keep in mind that one attorney should not represent several parties in a blended family, such as the mother, her children, and the stepfather. But most people don't want to pay three attorneys to iron out an estate plan. One way to guard against conflicts is to designate an independent third party to manage the assets that will be kept in trust for children but used during the lifetime of a stepparent.

STEPFAMILY FEUDS

HOW MESSY CAN things get when blended families go to settle estates? Fortunately most families who grapple with this can keep their differences relatively quiet and private. But the famous and ultrawealthy are not always so lucky. Two highly publicized cases demonstrate just how bad the postmortem battles can get.

Take the case of former *Playboy* model and topless stripper Anna Nicole Smith, who at age twenty-six became the bride of eighty-nine-year-old Texas oilman J. Howard Marshall, worth between $60 million and $1.6 billion. When he died a year later in 1995, a lengthy and public battle ensued between Smith, who at one point received $475 million from the estate, and Marshall's younger son, who thought she shouldn't have it. The court battles raged for more than seven years.

The other case involves the estate of Grateful Dead lead guitarist Jerry Garcia, who died of a heart attack in 1995 at age fifty-three. His free-spirited ways in life—five children, one widow, two ex-wives, one former mistress, and numerous former business associates—as well as his $10 million estate set the stage for a down-and-dirty materialistic mudfest when it came time to settle the estate. The litigation, which has dragged on more than seven years, has involved everything from Garcia's guitars to the royalties on his namesake "Cherry Garcia" ice cream, sold by Ben & Jerry's.

The saddest and perhaps most disconcerting thing about both cases is that each man did, in fact, have a will. Marshall left six wills and seven trust documents, none of which named Anna Nicole Smith. And Garcia had thoughtfully divvied up his estate into fifteenths for family members, with the largest share going to his widow. *Money* magazine even quoted an attorney who praised it as a model of thoughtful estate planning.

Animosity need not rule the day in all blended families. Several inheritors with whom I spoke clearly felt guilt, even responsibility, for the health and well-being of step-relatives after their parents had died. One woman who shared her father's inheritance with her siblings sent money to the daughter of his second wife because she fell on hard times after becoming ill with cancer. Two sisters whose father had remarried before his death seemed content to wait for their inheritance while the money sustained his widow, who had Alzheimer's, in a nice nursing home. One of the sisters even gave $10,000 to the girlfriend who kept him company after his wife went into the nursing home.

Family Business

Another area where estate planning poses a particular challenge is for families who own businesses. Much of the wealth streaming from the World War II generation is tied up in family businesses. Yet only one in three family-owned firms survive into the second generation and fewer than one in ten into the third. Whether the business lives on or dies with the founder often depends on how the estate planning is carried out, if at all. If the bulk of your family's estate is a business, whether a small ice cream shop or an international manufacturer, planning is critical if there is to be a successful transition of either ownership or wealth.

Families should start while the founder is still young to determine the best way to pass along assets, minimize estate taxes, and ensure a smooth succession, says Peg Eddy, a San Diego certified financial planner and cofounder of the Family Business Forum at the University of San Diego. Otherwise, in a worst-case scenario, the founder dies and no one in the family is prepared to take over. The business is sold and the children, who've never worked outside the family business, can't find other employment. "It can be devastating," says Eddy. "The legacy of that family is cut short."

FAMILY BUSINESS FACTS

- While the self-employed make up just 20 percent of the nation's workforce, they account for two-thirds of its millionaires. Their businesses, as paving contractors and mobile-home park owners, might not be glamorous, but they are profitable. The average millionaire is worth $3.7 million.[1]

- Why do family businesses fail? The three main reasons include lack of estate planning, failure to begin the transition to the next generation, and lack of money to pay estate taxes. In nearly 40 percent of the cases, the ultimate collapse of the firm was precipitated by the founder's death.[2]

- One-fourth of senior-generation family business share-holders have not completed any estate planning other than writing a will; 81 percent want the business to stay in the family; and 20 percent are not confident of the next generation's commitment to their business.[3]
- The average life span of the family-owned business is twenty-four years.[4]
- One of the potential advantages that successful privately held companies have over their public competitors is the ability to make long-term strategic decisions based, in part, on "patient capital," provided they have a unified shareholder group. Patient capital means they don't have to answer to securities analysts and outside investors, who tend to favor short-term results and shortsighted strategy.[5]

Business owners have a number of means to begin transferring ownership and control while they are alive. However, say the experts, the transfer still most commonly occurs at death. That's why it's important, if your parents run a family business, to begin discussing the following issues with them now.

Without proper planning a prosperous business can be subject to hefty estate taxes. Estate taxes are levied on the assets owned by a deceased person. For an individual, assets of up to $1 million are exempt from the taxes (in 2003; in 2004–2005, the exemption rises to $1.5 million). A married couple, however, can exempt $2 million if they set up a marital trust while both are living (or $3 million in 2004 and 2005). Above those exemption thresholds, estate taxes can climb as high as 49 percent.

Estate taxes must be paid to the Internal Revenue Service within nine months from the date of death—unless a closely held business accounts for at least 35 percent of the adjusted gross estate. In that case, the heirs can defer the estate taxes on the business portion of the estate. The heirs have four years to begin paying the taxes owed and can make the payments in annual installments over ten years. If the company is sold, however, the remaining taxes are due immediately. In many cases, says Eddy, the IRS will preclude the company making the payments from entering into a merger or making an acquisition. That's why people say, "I don't want to be in business with the IRS."

Although the IRS gives heirs time to raise the taxes and avoid liquidation, the payments can place a significant strain on the company, says Steven F. Carter, a certified financial planner. For instance, three of his clients are siblings trying to carry on the family's successful trucking company, but they are struggling to come up with $150,000 in annual estate tax installments. Carter says they feel constant financial pressure and have been forced to cut back on fringe benefits. "They are literally counting the years till they get out from under this burden," he says. "The kids are not enjoying the business as much as they did when dad was alive. Some simple planning five years ago would have eliminated all that."

But many business founders are independent, strong-willed people who don't like to confront their own mortality. "They're into control," says Eddy. "And they keep everything close to the vest." They have few outside hobbies and few retirement outlets. Some of them, says Eddy, even talk in terms of "*If* I die," rather than "when I die." So it can be a huge challenge for family members to sit them down and get them to discuss transition planning.

One woman who runs a Southern California contracting business with two hundred employees plans to pass the company to her three grown sons, but finds dealing with succession uncomfortable. She's hired an attorney and a psychologist to foster family communication, but admits she can take only so much at a time. Sometimes she feels like saying, "Why don't we stop talking about my dying?"

Eddy and other advisors say that a host of emotional issues can prevent planning a smooth transition: fear that a child will ruin the business, or, conversely, fear that the child will be more successful in running the company. There is also worry about being "fair" to each child.

If your family runs a business, you no doubt have some serious concerns yourself. Perhaps you want to run the real estate company. But Dad won't hand over the reins or insists on grooming your older brother, who would rather be a college sociology professor. Or maybe no one in your family wants to carry on your mom's successful restaurant, which she regards like another child. No one wants to discuss what will happen to the restaurant because it's like talking about a death.

"People think these are the soft, touchy-feely ideas,"

one CPA told me. "But we call those the hard issues. How would you like it if your daughter-in-law came up to you at a family gathering and said, 'You'll never see your grandchild again unless you make my husband president.' The tax stuff is almost easy."

FAMILIES WHO RUN businesses are increasingly calling upon psychologists to help them deal with the emotionally loaded issues of estate planning and succession. Company founders often put off planning because they fear that no one can replace them. "The thought of the business disintegrating is more than they can emotionally bear," says Alice B. Reinig, a San Diego psychologist and family business consultant.

Some business owners still believe in the old tradition of passing the firm on to the eldest son, even if he's not the most capable. Reinig says that sometimes the parent at the head of the company needs help recognizing that certain children aren't suited to the business roles they've been asked to play. Bringing in an outsider to run the company can be the best solution. Reinig has the family meet in the company boardroom rather than her office, so it doesn't smack of psychotherapy. All family members have a chance to speak. "It's really trying to help them manage conflict—within the business or without. If you can't have a successful family, you can't have a successful business."

The best way for your family to preserve the family business is in fact to begin giving part of it away to family members during life. Unfortunately, the thought of

giving away control even to their children terrifies some
business owners. One advisor encountered an owner who
had been to more than six attorneys, always hoping the
next would tell him he didn't need to begin transferring
to his heirs. If handled correctly, however, dealing with
questions of ownership and succession can actually
strengthen the relationship between parent and child, experts say. It takes courage and trust to let a child take over
a beloved business. "It is really something to see your
child pick up that baton and run," says Eddy. "It's almost
a spiritual thing."

Where business owners are willing to be flexible, there
is hope, says financial advisor Jeffrey Lipscomb. "There
are solutions to almost every problem."

Here are just some of the options:

- Keep the company in the founder's name and let it pass
  to the beneficiaries through the estate. Though a common method of transfer, it can create what planner
  Carter calls the worst of all possible worlds: a company
  passed from the male founder to his wife, who is not
  involved in the business, and run by the children, who
  have no ownership rights. "The spouse wants income
  and safety," says Carter. "The kids want to expand the
  business and open new markets." If the widow sells the
  company, the children are disenfranchised.
- Sell the company to its employees, who can include
  family members, using an Employee Stock Option
  Plan. The upside for the principals: If they sell at least
  one-third of the company stock and reinvest the pro-

ceeds in domestic stocks within twelve months, no capital gains taxes are owed. The downside: increased administrative chores and possible substantial costs.

- Sell to an outside business. This is an option when family members do not want to run the company. There are possible tax advantages: Sellers pay capital gains taxes, which are lower compared with estate taxes, which could run as high as 45 to 49 percent between 2003 and 2009 if the company is included in the estate during that period.

- Hire a manager from outside the family to run the company. In some cases it's better to hire a professional than cling to ownership of a company that's losing value from poor management.

- Give shares of the company to inheritors over time. Each individual can give $11,000 a year to any individual without generating gift taxes. A couple who owns a business and has three children could give a total of $22,000 to each annually. The shares given as a gift appreciate in value outside of the estate—and are beyond the reach of estate taxes. However, should the heirs sell their interest, they could incur sizable capital gains taxes.

- Sell shares to their children and grandchildren over time. The inheritors could use their own money or gifted money. Again, these shares appreciate outside of the estate.

It is essential, however, that the parents' interest in the company exceed 35 percent of their total estate to qualify for the ten-year estate-tax installment plan.

- Create two classes of stock ownership, preferred and common. The founder holds the preferred, which remains part of the estate. But the value is then frozen and the "appreciation clock" stops. The common stock is distributed to successors and continues to appreciate. But this method can be tricky. Work with an attorney and accountant who are up to speed on the latest IRS rules.
- Establish a family limited partnership, which many experts consider an excellent tool. Parents can gradually pass units of ownership to their beneficiaries while maintaining control and receiving income. And the IRS allows the units to be valued at a discount—which helps avoid estate tax.

  The IRS might consider a $1 million business to be worth only $800,000 if it is held by a limited partnership, because the ownership is not readily marketable. If the ownership is spread among several family members, the IRS could also acknowledge a "lack of control" discount, further lowering value to $650,000. Limited partnerships can be employed for all kinds of assets, such as real estate and stock portfolios, not just family businesses.
- Use life insurance to provide liquidity for the estate. Life insurance passed through an estate is subject to estate taxes. Set up outside the estate, it can be a highly useful source of tax-free cash. Here are two examples of that strategy:

  1. The founder could set up an irrevocable life insurance trust. At his or her death, the proceeds would

go to the trust beneficiaries, say children and grand-children. Such trusts cannot be attached by lawsuits or divorcing spouses.

2. Life insurance can also fund a buy-sell agreement between principal owners. Let's say your father and his partner own a construction company. They each take out a life insurance policy on the other. Should your father die first, the insurance would be used to buy your father's share from your mother (or his benefici-aries), leaving his partner with the company and your family with cash rather than an illiquid asset.

These arrangements can have substantial tax conse-quences, and professional advice is needed in choosing a game plan.

Keep in mind that one strategy alone is unlikely to get the job done. Most situations require several approaches to create an integrated plan. Even then, no plan is likely to be perfect or to anticipate every situation.

THE BOSSES' SONS

WHEN IT COMES to estate and succession planning, leading family-business advisor Peg Eddy practices what she preaches. She and her husband, Bob, founded their own business, Creative Capital Management Inc., in San Diego in the mid-1970s. The Eddys have always made it clear to their two grown sons that if they want to join the family business they'll have to earn their way in.

To be hired at the firm each would have to meet the fol-lowing requirements: get a college degree, work three to five years at another company and earn at least one promotion, apply when there's an opening like anyone else. Once at the company they would report to someone other than a parent. Or they could offer to buy the business. Both sons sit on the board of directors. At least twice a year, the parents ask formally whether they're interested in joining the business. To date, they've said no. And that's okay, says Eddy. She's met too many forty-year-old men going through midlife crises because all they've ever done is work for the family company. The two young men also have copies of their parents' estate plan and are familiar with their finances.

What's fair is not always equal. When the bulk of an estate is comprised of a family business, dividing the inheritance equally among heirs can be a great challenge. Sometimes the business is left to the children who want to run it, while those who don't get other assets or insurance proceeds of equal value. But heirs can still feel shortchanged, depending on circumstances. Eddy recalls the case of a young man who inherited the family business, while his sister got cash. At first the business had cash-flow problems and the brother resented his sister's living on "easy street." But then the financial tables turned. The business began to prosper, and now he's better off.

Reinig, the family business consultant, knows of one family that successfully divided the inherited business into three companies, with each of the three children running one. In another instance, when the founder of a farm equipment dealership began planning for his succession, recalls Muscio, the man considered his three children, who all worked in the business. However, he decided to give the company away in four equal shares—one each to his children and one to his daughter's ex-husband, who was clearly the most able successor. Despite its unusual nature, the arrangement suited everyone just fine. The ex–son-in-law worked hard, kept the business growing, and made the biggest salary. The three children continued working there, but were happy with their less-demanding jobs.

Chapter 4

Death of a Parent

*No matter what our age, the death of a parent is
devastating; nothing leaves us feeling so abandoned. It
means saying goodbye to the people who gave us life.*
—Fiona Marshall, *Losing a Parent: Practical Help for You
and Other Family Members*

A chapter on grief might seem off the point in a
book on managing an inheritance. But I have
found in my interviews with heirs that their grief
can greatly influence the decisions they make about their
bequests. Many people feel embarrassed or ashamed to
mourn for their parents beyond a few months. And when
they try to contain these feelings, they pop up in unexpected ways while dealing with the parent's legacy. (See
Chapter 7, From the Grave). Recognizing the depth of
their grief and acknowledging that it will take time to
cope can, I hope, help survivors move on.

After my mother died, I began to think of myself as an
orphan, even though that description seemed melodra-
matic to me. After all, I was not some Dickensian protag-
onist, bereft and all alone in the world. I was thirty-nine

years old with a husband and two children of my own. But my relationships with them were different from the one I had with my mother. They had never known me as a child and didn't my share a big portion of my life's history.

A Multitude of Orphans

For years, I'd just assumed that my feelings of orphanhood stemmed from the fact I'm an only child. I was surprised when I recently discovered that this feeling is widespread among adults who've lost parents, whether they are from large or small families. On a visit to my local bookstore I found a section on grieving and within that an entire shelf devoted to the loss of parents. The books had names like *Midlife Orphan: Facing Life's Changes Now that Your Parents Are Gone* and *The Orphaned Adult: Confronting the Death of a Parent*. The subject of becoming an orphan is at the core of Dave Eggers's bestselling *A Heartbreaking Work of Staggering Genius*, a searing memoir about losing both his parents while in his early twenties.

"When my mom died, I felt like an orphan," a woman in her fifties named Laura told me. "I felt totally alone." Laura's mother had kept Laura's wedding dress from her first marriage, thirty years before. "I can't throw that away," she said. "What am I going to do with it?" Laura would like to display her mother's collection of thimbles, but hasn't yet found the motivation. She took some black-and-white family photographs to a "creative memory" scrapbook class several times, but each time she would have to leave partway through. "I would just be in tears. I still haven't finished it."

When the Second Parent Dies

Losing one parent is a sad occasion. But losing both can be a major life event, a rite of passage to mature adulthood. "Few of us are prepared for the intensity or the duration of our grief," writes Jane Brooks in *Midlife Orphan*. "The death of the last parent, an event that we've known would obviously happen someday, is a shock to our core in ways that we have not anticipated."

Losing both your parents means that you're nobody's child anymore. This can be a blow whether you're eighteen or eighty-one. Your place in the universe has shifted as well. You'll be the next one to get old, the next one to die. As Susan Kane, a *New York* magazine editor, put it, "Your parents' deaths are going to leave this yawning gap between you and eternity."

Kane, who edits *Babytalk* magazine, described in the May 2001 issue how the death of her father prompted her to reexperience the loss of her mother:

> Friends had warned me that losing the second parent would make me grieve anew for the first, but I don't think I was prepared for just how true that was. This morning as I walked to work I was feeling stressed; I'm settling my dad's affairs and trying to be a good editor and wife and mom all at once. Suddenly I could vividly imagine my mom's voice comforting me, and the hugeness of the loss of her almost overwhelmed

me. I literally felt that I was going to fall down. My mother couldn't bear it when I was unhappy. I can still hear how concerned her voice would become, how she would suggest a million ways to make it better. How even when I was in my thirties she would call me her "Susiebelle" in a voice so drenched with love I feel my heart will break just remembering it.

Long-distance Caregiving

Adding to the great sadness of losing a parent is the physical and emotional trauma some adult children suffer caring for a dying mother or father. Increased longevity and improved medical care often mean a long, tortuous decline for a frail parent. The adult children might spend those finals months on a roller-coaster ride, up and down, careening from a dying parent in another state to home and family, and back again.

When I called her, Kane shared the story of her harried last months with her father. He needed full-time care, but wouldn't accept any help, even housecleaning. So she and her two sisters, all of whom lived a plane ride away, would take turns visiting him. Because he had stopped opening his mail, his bills were going unpaid. The house had fallen into disrepair. On one occasion Kane hurriedly arrived at father's home to take him for a doctor's appointment, but couldn't work his portable oxygen equipment. They ended up going to the emergency room as a code blue, with attendants flying to the gurney just like on television.

This story sounded all too familiar to me. Because I

also had young children, I could not focus all my time and energy on my mother in her final months. For the eighteen months my mother was terminally ill, I often felt that I was living a nightmare. When people are distraught, when time is precious, and everyone is in a hurry, bad things will happen. At one point both my mother and my one-year-old son were taken to the same hospital within minutes of each other.

I was preparing to admit my mother to the hospital for tests for severe stomach pain. Then I received a call that my son was en route to the ER by ambulance. He had been accidentally locked in a sweltering car by our beloved baby-sitter, distraught over how sick my mother was. The fire department had used an ax to break the car window and remove my son, whose temperature had climbed above 105 degrees in less than ten minutes. My mother turned out to have gallstones and returned home the next day. The baby recovered quickly. But the baby-sitter and I are likely to have flashbacks for the rest of our lives.

Although that was the most horrific incident from that period, events never seemed to go smoothly. At one point my mother, who had been staying with us in California, decided she was well enough to go home to El Paso. But she was soon gravely ill again, and too sick to transport back to California except by air ambulance, which she didn't want to do. She entered one hospital, then was transferred by mistake to another, an old rundown facility with limited staffing, and couldn't be transferred to a better one without losing Medicare benefits. Every day at work, I would leave my desk, walk along a glassed-in catwalk adjoining the newspaper building in which I worked, and call her at the hospital from a pay phone. I felt terribly guilty that she was dying hundreds of miles away from me all alone and I couldn't leave my young children and my job to be with her. The last thing she ever said to me one dark rainy January afternoon was, "Get me out of here."

Looking for Good Endings

My point in sharing these stories is to show how hard it is to shake these pervasive feelings of grief and guilt. Because grown children now commonly live far away from their parents, it's easy to feel that we're always out of position, never in time for those final days and hours. Fortunately, there's been a lot written about dying in the last thirty years, which has made it easier for us to discuss. But one aspect of this disturbs me. You could call it the "good death" movement, which leads people to believe that it's possible to arrange for their loved ones to have a comfortable, peaceful death and that those who share it will have a noble and purifying experience.

However, those of us with messier, more unpleasant endings feel that we've somehow failed to arrange things correctly. But as, Brooks notes, "The truth is, death is rarely beautiful. In our society, more often than not, death means tubes, machines, or, at the very least, painkillers that anesthetize not only the pain but also the personality." Brooks's own mother was fearful of dying and would cry out to her—don't let me die! Brooks wished that her mother would be more heroic, like in the movies.

Another aspect of modern life that engenders regret in those dealing with death is the pervasive lack of ritual. If your parents, like mine, were not religious, you could find yourself wishing for the comfort of prescribed ceremonies and methods of mourning. It's important to have an opportunity to say good-bye, to share your grief with others, and to gain a sense of finality. If your family has never participated in a religion, it's hard to suddenly adopt one.

You might want to devise some rituals of your own. My husband helped me to do just that when my mother died. Knowing that she did not want a funeral, he suggested an alternative that would help comfort me. We decided to have a reception at my mother's home. My husband urged me to find some photographs of my mother at different times in her life and display them on the mantel in the living room. The guests enjoyed being in her sunny living room one last time and talking with me about the pictures. For me, it provided a welcome substitute for a more formal ceremony, the comfort of seeing her friends and neighbors, and a necessary sense of finality.

San Diego psychiatrist Dr. Susan Erman says most people are helped by having rituals to follow when a loved one dies. Erman, who is Jewish, says her religion has a prescribed method of mourning: an immediate burial, a period of bereavement at home, then steps to follow for the remainder of the first year. And it usually takes about a year, she says, for most people to emerge from a period of grieving. If it does take more than a year, many therapists say, you might need additional help.

But grieving doesn't confine itself to set periods of mourning. "It can happen in pieces," says Olivia Mellan, a psychologist and author. "It doesn't happen all at once." I still vividly remember a few months after my father's death, standing and holding a strap riding the subway in New York City, where I was attending graduate school. I started to think about him and suddenly tears were splashing down my face and onto the floor. I had no tissues to stop the flow. Other passengers politely pretended not to notice.

If you need time to reflect and mourn, Mellan recommends creating your own rituals. Place photographs in a special place, write letters. "Light candles," says Mellan. "Talk to the person."

Do men and women mourn differently? Yes, says Mellan, they tend to react differently, much as they do during divorce. Men are less likely to be in touch with their feelings in the first place. They tend to compartmentalize their mourning and move on. Women, however, take the emotional impact head-on, suffering openly, talking about their feelings.

You'll know you are recovering from your grieving, according to Helen Fitzgerald, author of *The Mourning Handbook: A Complete Guide for the Bereaved*, when you no longer feel tired all the time; your eating, sleeping, and exercise patterns begin to return to normal; and you can enjoy time alone. You can also plan and organize for your future.

Sometimes, a Surprising Sense of Liberation

For her book *Losing Your Parents, Finding Your Self: The Defining Turning Point of Adult Life*, author Victoria Secunda surveyed ninety-four men and women who had lost one or both parents as adults to learn the impact on them. She found that the impact was significant, often prompting a change in relations with the surviving parents, siblings, and spouses. The removal of one family member usually forces a realignment within the family that can either strengthen or weaken existing ties.

The results can be surprising. With parents gone, siblings who had sparred vigorously for attention might find themselves at peace with one another. The loss of one parent can have a big effect as well on a surviving child's marriage. I know of one woman in her fifties who had long had a difficult marriage and delivered a daily blow-by-blow account of her husband's shortcomings to her mother, who in turn made known her disapproval of her son-in-law. The mother's death, after a long illness, seemed to have a salutary effect on the daughter and on her marriage. A divisive force within their relationship was gone. With counseling, the couple enjoyed a renewed commitment and affection.

"Far from being an insignificant event, parental death is *the* milestone—provides *the* indelible line of demarcation—that enables adult offspring to begin to determine whether or not they are, or still must learn how to be truly grown up."

—VICTORIA SECUNDA

Though we might prefer to avoid it at first, taking on the mantle of adulthood is not all bad. While we can no longer win our parents' approval, we can't incur their disapproval either. We are freer to do what we want, how we want. And if we've received an inheritance, we might have the means to carry out our life's goals. In his book, *The Orphaned Adult*, Alexander Levy notes, "There is a kind of liberation associated with the deaths of parents in addition to the disorientation and sorrow they impart."

In her survey, Secunda found that the biggest changes adult orphans made was in their careers. Half stated they had made a career change since a parent's death, and of those, 70 percent said the changes were a direct result of the deaths. The reasons varied, however. The passing of a parent prompted some to reevaluate what they wanted to do for the remainder of the working lives, others felt they had better control of their own destinies, and still others felt they could shed the dreams and ambitions their parents had for them.

One such woman was Susan, who graduated from one of the top law schools in the country. But her heart never seemed to be in the practice of law. She had no desire to work the killer hours or play the office politics necessary to be made a partner. Nor did Susan like the confrontational, adversarial aspects of the law. She tended to change firms every few years, always searching for a job that met her values. But once her father died, she realized she no longer felt obligated to continue in the career he'd wanted for her. Finally, after several years, she decided to go back to school to pursue a career as a law librarian, something that suited her quiet, contemplative personality.

If we no longer have someone to blame for making us do something, we also have no one to blame for holding us back. Peg Eddy, president of Creative Capital Management in San Diego, says, "Not until both parents die do we get beyond arrested adolescence. There's only so long you can complain about who your parents are and what they've done to you."

Take the Baton and Run

Dealing with your parents' deaths and their estates can force you to find inner strength you didn't know you had. When I was having a particularly difficult time with a supervisor at work, I remember thinking often about those months of caring for my mother and family. While the office situation was bad, I had been through much worse, I told myself. If I endured all that suffering, I could certainly get through this. I'd find a way to survive. And I did.

Those years of balancing work, young children, a dying mother, and a new inheritance forever helped focus my attention on what's important. I've learned to practice triage with any crisis that comes my way. All human beings related to me get top priority. Broken cars can be fixed, missed appointments can be rescheduled, late bills can be paid later. Even now when I shift into my "this too shall pass" mode, friends will comment on my seeming calm in the midst of stressful events.

Dealing with doctors, making life-and-death decisions, handling large sums of money, realizing what a lifetime adds up to can spur you to go after what's important to you "before it's too late." My mother died when I was thirty-nine. When I turned forty, my predominant thought was that my life was probably half over. I had reached a now-or-never moment. Was I going to accomplish all that I wanted?

"Death is one deadline that no one is anxious to meet," writes Jane Brooks in *Midlife Orphan*. "Yet, it is when we have a deadline that we often accomplish the most. It's what nudges us on, pushing us to explore and to experiment while we have the opportunity. In the face of the deadline brought to our attention by our last parent's death, we find ourselves turning outward with renewed purpose and vigor. After all, there is much to do and no time to waste."

You might be determined, after the death of a parent, to take care of unfinished business or pursue a long-held dream. But unlike many people, you have an inheritance that could help underwrite that dream. Your job will be to manage your gift wisely while you work through your emotions. Start with the next chapter.

Chapter 5

Becoming an Inheritor

To heir is human.
(With apologies to Alexander Pope)

The days and weeks following the death of a parent are likely to be harried and stressful. Unfortunately, many financial and legal tasks require your attention. But they need not become overwhelming. "Get over the funeral," says estate planning attorney Nancy A. Spector. "Take some time to grieve. Some people dive in and want to wrap it up right away, but very rarely is it an emergency situation."

Here's how to get started:

- Locate the will or trust. Identify the executor of the will or the trustee of the trust. Determine heirs and beneficiaries.
- Review the will and trust documents carefully. Be certain that you understand them.
- Even with detailed estate plans, you need to work with

an attorney experienced in probate and estate planning, either the one who prepared your parent's estate plan or one of your own choosing. Don't hesitate to ask exactly how you will be charged, by the hour or on a flat-fee basis. And don't be embarrassed to look cost-conscious even though you are grieving.

- If your parent left a will, it most likely names an executor to carry out the will's instructions. A similar duty is performed by the trustee, if the deceased left an estate in trust. The duties of the executor and trustee typically include locating all beneficiaries (any person or organization entitled to receive gifts made through a will or trust), inventorying the assets, and ensuring that the beneficiaries don't receive any money until all debts including any estate taxes are paid off, says Spector. No one wants to be running after beneficiaries who've been paid already to collect money for bills that have not.

- If your parent died intestate, that is, without a will, you should consult an attorney. The estate will likely have to go through a court procedure known as probate. The assets will be distributed according to state law, based on the family relationship of heirs to the parent. While many people try to avoid probate because of its inflexibility, inconvenience, and costs for attorney fees, it can be beneficial if heirs are feuding.

- Locate and open any safe deposit boxes. Take inventory.

- For insurance and annuity benefits, call and obtain the proper documents to collect the proceeds if you are designated the beneficiary.

- Establish a workplace. If you are the executor, clear an area in your home to use as your headquarters for settling the estate. Keep all files and relevant documents there. Even a modest estate can generate considerable paperwork, from such sources as Social Security, banks, investments, and pensions.
- Put it in writing. Whenever you talk with anyone associated with your parent's estate, keep careful notes, especially of the names and phone numbers of the people with whom you spoke. Although you might feel you're coping well after your loss, you could find later that you have significant gaps in your recollections of technical or legal details. It's not at all uncommon for heirs to essentially sleepwalk their way through important conversations during this time. Should someone call you on a significant matter that doesn't require an immediate response when you're having a bad day, simply say you need to talk at another time. Don't feel obligated to put on a brave face.
- Keep a notebook and pen by the telephone to keep a log of all calls relating to the estate and notes about each.
- Order death certificates. A death certificate, the official record of an individual's death, lists the person's name, Social Security number, date of birth, and cause of death. As you deal with insurance companies, investment firms, and federal agencies, you will need to give each one proof of death with a certified copy of the death certificate.

    Some estates may require as many as twenty copies. In my mother's case, I initially ordered six, then had to order that many again. Just consider all the different entities that are likely to request a copy: Social Security, Veterans Affairs, pension administrator, insurance companies, health insurers, banks, brokerage houses, credit card companies, and real estate title companies. As a rule of thumb, I recommend estimating how many you think you need, then doubling it. Many mortuaries will order death certificates for you as a service and pass along the cost in your bill, which can be a great convenience. Obtaining them from the local vital statistics office or county recorder takes longer and usually involves more effort.

- Collect and carefully scrutinize the mail. If you're having trouble locating all of your parent's assets, what comes in the mail should eventually alert you to them. If you live elsewhere, have all mail forwarded to you. Consider that your loved one might have been unfamiliar with certain benefits. My mother had never mentioned that her teacher's annuity carried a $10,000 benefit, probably because she didn't know herself or had forgotten. I only found out about it when I called the Texas teacher's pension system, from which she received a monthly pension, to say that she had passed away and ask what I should do next.

- Cancel credit cards and subscriptions. It's not enough that your parent's credit cards stop being used. In this age of identity theft, it's important to call each card issuer and ask how to close the account officially. Some consumer organizations recommend you cut up and return the card as well.

- Determine any debts. These could include medical

bills, property taxes, income taxes, liens, and credit card debts. Any such debts should be paid by the estate, prior to beneficiaries receiving their payments. (However, if the debts exceed the assets in the estate, family members are not required by law to repay them.) When funds are available, pay debts with top priority, such as mortgages and taxes.

- List all assets and estimate the value of each:

Real estate
Bank accounts
Cash and money market funds
Promissory notes
401(k)s and IRAs
Stocks and bonds (either individual or in mutual funds)
Motor vehicles
Antiques and collectibles
Business interests
Copyrights
Household and miscellaneous items

A word of caution: Be careful when dealing with inherited IRAs. If handled correctly, they can live on after your parent has died, providing substantial value for you and your beneficiaries. But your parent must have named individuals or a trust (not the estate) as primary and secondary beneficiaries. If you are the beneficiary of an IRA, you do not have to withdraw all the money at once, thereby losing the tax-deferred advantage. You can keep it as an IRA and take small, annual withdrawals based upon your life expectancy, which could be several decades. Meanwhile, it could continue to earn and grow. To preserve this valuable asset, you must never transfer it into your own IRA account. Keep it in the original owner's name and have the account custodian add your name and Social Security number. You can, however, change the investment mix and the custodian, through a custodian-to-custodian transfer. The IRA that I inherited from my mother is now titled "Ann Hoffman Perry as Beneficiary of Cordelia B. Hoffman."

• Prepare and file a final income tax return for your parent or loved one.

Settling an estate can be daunting if family members keep their beneficiaries ignorant of their affairs. Kent Hickey, a certified financial planner in Allentown, Pennsylvania, shared the story of this asset scavenger hunt. Dad was of the Depression era and did not believe women needed to know about finances. He was so worried about another Depression that he had five safe deposit boxes in five different banks, CDs at a variety of financial institutions, and a slew of government bonds purchased over decades. Though he didn't lose any money during his life, says Hickey, he saddled his daughter with a lot of needless hassle and expense in hiring advisors to help find the assets.

Just sorting through decades' worth of another person's paperwork is enough to drive most people to distraction. After her father died, editor Susan Kane got a request from the IRS to verify his Social Security number on a prior tax return. It turned out to be off by one digit. "It took me five hours to go through the boxes and find the return," she says. "I remember just weeping, absolutely weeping, thinking: when is this going to end?" Kane was the executor of her father's estate and found that pulling it all together to meet probate deadlines was stressful: "It's not as simple as ashes to ashes, dust to dust. My God, people's lives are complicated."

CASHING OUT

MANY OLDER PEOPLE have a tendency to stash assets, as I discussed in Chapter 2, Planning Together, but sometimes their habits can become extreme. One day after my mother retired, a friend of hers dropped by her house. Nancy, who was from out of town, was cleaning out the home of her elderly mother, an antique collector who had just passed away. Of course, Nancy had expected to inherit the many valuable treasures displayed throughout the house. What she didn't expect was to find $20 bills tucked in every nook, cranny, and book. Nancy had come to ask my mother's help in sorting it all out. They hurried back to Nancy's mother's house, closed the curtains, and sat on the floor counting. They counted and counted and counted—more than $70,000. Nancy felt suddenly much more prosperous. And my mother had the distinct impression that Nancy wasn't about to share the secret with other family members or the IRS.

I've occasionally been asked by readers who've received large inheritances whether they don't owe some kind of tax on it. The answer is probably not. This is a common source of confusion, however. If you are suddenly $800,000 richer, it seems that you must owe the government something.

Here's how it works. Federal estate taxes are assessed on the estate itself. So, if your benefactor's wealth exceeded the limit, the tax was paid before you received your bequest. Your gift was not income, so you do not owe income taxes (not yet anyway!). In some states, you could owe state inheritance tax, which is paid by the inheritor, depending on the relationship to the benefactor.

A Big Break

When you inherit stocks, real estate, or items that can appreciate, you could get a huge tax break—known as a "step-up in basis." Basis is the value of an asset for tax purposes. That means if you inherit stock in Heir Apparent Inc. worth $100,000 at the time of your benefactor's death, your "basis" for calculating future capital gains is $100,000, not the $20,000 your father paid for it. If you sell some or all of that stock immediately upon receiving it, you'll owe no capital gains tax. The long-term (held for at least one year and a day) capital gains rate is 20 percent for those in the higher tax brackets; for the lowest two brackets, the 10 and 15 percent brackets, the rate is 10 percent.

The best time to sell an asset that can appreciate is often immediately after it's inherited, say financial advisors. The step-up in basis essentially turns assets such as stocks and real estate into cash, as long as they're sold soon after the benefactor's death. This is a great opportunity for heirs to diversify what they're received and insulate themselves from risk. Unfortunately, however, selling off part of the estate soon after the death is emotionally difficult for many inheritors.

It's a good idea to have any property or valuable assets other than stocks and bonds appraised soon after your parent's death whether or not you plan to sell right away. The appraisal serves as your basis for capital gains, a valuation for insurance, and also as a reality check. When I had our cabin in Michigan appraised a few months after my mother died, it was valued at $160,000. My mother and I had guessed it might be worth $80,000, unaware of the recent surge in demand for lakefront property no matter how small the parcel. The market value is useful to know so the cabin can be properly insured and so we can accurately gauge how it fits in with our long-range plans. And if some emergency forced us to sell, we would use the appraisal to calculate our capital gain (the selling price minus the appraised price at my mother's death).

I also had the large painting that hung in our family home appraised, not knowing what to expect. The appraiser pegged it at $8,000. I was pleased to have our good taste validated, but I also immediately had it insured before it made the trip to California.

My mother never had any idea the painting in the living room had value. That's why it's a good idea to find a trusted appraiser or consignment shop owner who can help you determine if you have any unknown treasures. When a friend of mine was sorting through her late mother's possessions, she recognized a certain pot. It was one she'd known all through childhood, but also one of a type she'd recently heard discussed on "Antiques Roadshow," worth almost $2,000.

The oddest items can be valuable, says Peggy Russ, my neighbor and a former consignment store owner. "Something as silly as duck decoys, depending on who carved them, could be worth $2,000 each. People give away first editions and signed books all the time. And they're worth a ton of money." Because collectibles are so varied and no one appraiser is familiar with all categories, Russ recommends going online to eBay and other sites to check whether you might have something of value.

STOCK SLEUTHING

IF YOU FIND old stock certificates curled up in your parents' desk drawer or gathering dust in the garage, resist the urge to toss them or use them to wallpaper the basement. These often colorful and ornately drawn certificates could have value—either as stocks or as collectibles. When I found thirty-three shares of an obscure Canadian mining company in my parents' safe deposit box in 1993, I was stumped, but also curious. A note, dated May 1, 1949, to my father from a relative named Marian, said: "This stock has no value that I know of. You can keep it in case it would in the future." Well, I was hooked. I tried tracking it down on my own, but had no luck. Finally I turned to the professional firm of Stock Search International, paid a $75 fee, and agreed to give them 30 percent of whatever family fortune they uncovered. Alas, there was no fortune to share. The shares of Kir-Vit Mines Limited were of no value, not even as collectibles. So why bother checking? Stock Search says that while 60 percent of old certificates, like mine, have no value, 20 percent have collector's value, 10 percent have money value, and another 10 percent have potential value, after a bankruptcy or reorganization.

Bill, a Texas attorney, remembers how difficult it was working from afar to get his late father's house, which had fallen into disrepair, ready to go on the market. The house, in another state, needed a new roof, floors, and paint. With his father's illness, he says, "We hadn't really paid attention to the house. We had kept it together with Band-Aids." Once work began, he says, "It was really hard getting those calls and e-mails all day." But eventually, when spruced up, the house sold for more than the asking price.

Before I sold my parents' home, I opted to have the basement shored up even though it wasn't necessary in order to sell it. I just didn't want to be confronted with any problems once I had finally said good-bye. My biggest regret about getting the house ready was how little time I gave myself to sort everything into the "keep" and "give away" piles. I tried to do it all in one long weekend when I had the flu. As a result, I ended up with my mother's half-used spice jars and box of Hefty trash bags, but foolishly gave away my childhood piano music. And I didn't do enough to ensure that a World War II footlocker got put on the moving van. Until that final cleanup, I hadn't known it was in the basement. It belonged to my mother's beloved brother, a young fighter pilot shot down over Germany. I never even got to look inside.

Wild Cards

There will occasionally be the loose end or odd asset that needs your attention. When working with my mother on her estate plan, it didn't occur to either of us to include the rights to Go Fish because the game had not been manufactured for several years. I didn't give it any thought until a few years after her death, when my neighbors informed me that a detective had contacted them looking for me. The detective had been hired by a major hotel chain planning a television commercial that made reference to the game of Go Fish. The company wanted to pay a few thousand dollars to ensure that I wouldn't sue them for copyright infringement. Working with an attorney in California and another in Texas, we quickly had the rights transferred from my mother's name to mine.

Figuring out what to do in that case was fairly simple. But sometimes you just have to wing it, as my mother and I had to do in one case after my father's death. It turned out that he had used some of the money left to him by his mother, about $23,000, to lend at high rates to a company, Jardinas de Tlalnepantla, developing Mexican cemeteries. And that wasn't the worst. The "gardens" no longer smelled so sweet and were in bankruptcy. We were stymied. Even if we could find someone to help us learn more about the situation, we might have to pay thousands out of pocket and still not recover the money. Then one day a letter came from an attorney in Mexico who purportedly was helping investors get back their money from the bankrupt company for a portion of the amount recovered. Though we worried that the attorney might be on the take or in league somehow with the company, we decided to do it, figuring the attorney couldn't get paid unless he produced. To our amazement we eventually received about $15,000, minus the attorney's fee.

Go Fish Heiress Dos and Don'ts

Every inheritance is different, depending on the size and the kind of assets. And each inheritor's response is unique, depending on personality and feelings about the benefactor. Inheritors are often bombarded with advice from family, friends, wanna-be advisors, and even from the grave. But there are a few simple rules that will help inheritors keep their bequest "heir-tight." Anyone who's received an inheritance, no matter how modest, should proceed carefully and cautiously. Based on my own experience and that of the many financial advisors I consult, here are the nine rules to avoid blowing an inheritance:

1. Don't rush into any major decisions, such as selling a home or family heirloom. And don't feel you must make important investment choices quickly. A money

market fund is often the best place for cash to reside until you are ready to develop a financial plan. Some financial advisors or relatives will try to hurry you. Resist this. Some may have your best interests at heart, while others could be driven by profit motive. Some friends and relatives seem to get vicarious excitement from trying to manage someone else's money. But it's not theirs, it's yours. Responding to an urgency to invest is a mistake. You need to understand how your life has changed first, then proceed with caution.

2. Resist the urge to give part away. People sometimes feel uncomfortable or guilty having more than others and, thus, unconsciously want to cast it off. Unfortunately, the smell of a large sum of money brings out everyone you've ever known with a sad story or great investment idea. Rose, a Midwestern insurance broker, received an insurance payout when her young husband died. She remembers feeling undeserving. "I felt guilty that I had so much when we had had so little," she says. She gave most of it away. A financial consultant who specializes in helping widows was stunned when his widowed mother informed him she'd given half her recent $400,000 inheritance to the consultant's spendthrift brother. This was a situation he'd seen all too often in his work—elderly women who felt they could not say "no" to their grown children. How should you reply if you are hit up for money? You can say you need it for your financial security. Or, as one advisor to wealthy clients recommends, "I care too much about you to complicate our relationship with an investment."

3. Be certain all property and valuables are safe and insured. While I cared for my mother in our California home, her home in Texas was unoccupied. It was burglarized twice before we installed an alarm. Though the losses were minimal, the sense of violation at that emotional time was painful. Just a few days after my husband's mother died, her home in Northern California was flooded in the El Niño winter storms. We had all been so focused on her and her health that we didn't think much about the house. I had even bought flood insurance on our home, but not for hers, which was prone to flooding. Insurance wouldn't have prevented the flood, but it would have made dealing with the sad scene easier and less costly.

4. Don't make any sudden changes such as moving to another city or quitting your job. You need some time to get comfortable with the money, so you can make a rational decision. For the first few months or years, you are likely to be more susceptible to emotions.

5. Allow time for grieving. Recognize that depression can cloud your judgment and seek professional help if the problem lingers. Grief can strike months or years after you think you should be "over it."

6. Even in community property states, your inheritance belongs to you alone unless you take steps to share it with your spouse. An inheritance can change the dynamics of a relationship, so be sensitive to your partner's feelings. (For more, see Chapter 8, Yours, Mine, or Ours?)

7. Consider treating yourself to a small portion of the

inheritance. Financial advisors say most heirs are bound to do this anyway, so it's best to acknowledge it up front and set limits. Spending 5 or 10 percent of the bequest can act as a safety valve that prevents inheritors from splurging it all. Several months after my mother passed away, my faithful Toyota subcompact needed replacing. I paid $23,000 cash for a new minivan (I'll always remember the startled look on the salesman's face when he asked how I wanted to finance it and I wrote out a check for the entire amount). I wanted to help my family heal after many months of emotional trauma, and the idea of a van for family outings and transporting kids to sports and play practices seemed to fit the bill. Nine years and 152,000 miles later, I still consider it a righteous splurge. In retrospect, this was a good thing for another reason. It marked the first time I used the money for myself. It was the beginning of my new relationship with this money. I had control over it.

8. Consult the experts. Depending on the complexity of your inheritance, you could need a financial planner, accountant, attorney, pension expert, insurance broker, and even an appraiser for special collections. Often one expert, such as a planner, can serve as your financial quarterback. (See Chapter 11, Getting Professional Help.)

9. Do your own estate planning, knowing that you have more to leave your heirs now and that a thoughtfully planned estate is a gift in itself. (See Chapter 13, Planning Your Own Estate.)

Chapter 6

Mixed Blessings

———

*The great American sin is having advantage
without earning it.*
—Paul G. Schervish, director, Social Welfare Research
Institute at Boston College

I t wasn't long after I received my inheritance that I
found myself working on a column for my newspaper about a fascinating organization called More
Than Money, a support group for heirs that encourages
them to practice philanthropy. It also provides counseling
for heirs experiencing problems with their new wealth.
During a telephone interview, the group's spokesman,
Allen Hancock, told me that the $500,000 he'd received
at age twenty-two from his grandfather was both a blessing and a burden.

Hancock said he was pleased that he could live comfortably off the bequest and was free to volunteer for cul-
tural and social causes. But he felt isolated sometimes and
guilty that he had so much when others had so little. As
the years passed, he found ways to come to terms with his
bequest.

"I found it important to 'come out' and tell people that I'm an inheritor and how much I've inherited," he told me. "It wasn't easy. I started slowly, by telling a couple of close friends. But I've found it liberating."

Listening to Hancock speak, I was suddenly energized. I remember crouching in the corner of my newsroom cubicle, hand cupped over the receiver, telling this pleasant stranger on the telephone things I'd never shared with my longtime colleagues sitting ten feet away from me.

"I'm an inheritor, too," I whispered. "The same as you, $500,000." I told him that I felt isolated as well. While not large, my inheritance was big enough to change other people's perceptions of me and I had no control over that. So I simply kept it a secret. If word leaked out at work, would I ever again get a raise (and the pat on the back that goes with it)? Would friends, relatives, and colleagues resent me if I shared details of my good fortune? And would any of them be sympathetic to the problems of settling an estate?

I'm sure it was one of the more unusual "interviews" that Hancock gave to the media. But at the end of it, I felt a great sense of relief. I wasn't the only one to feel burdened by something the rest of the world regarded as a blessing.

Beyond the Daydream Image

Most people, naturally, regard receiving an inheritance as a pleasant daydream come true. But heirs often find it a mixed blessing. One man who inherited a seven-figure estate wrote me, "On the one hand, you are ecstatic with attaining a measure of financial security. On the other hand, well, there are many other issues; children with no grandparents, lost loved ones, fear of doing something stupid with the assets, IRS, attorneys, on it goes."

Michael Stolper, whose Stolper & Co. in San Diego helps wealthy clients across the country manage their money, says an inheritance doesn't have to be large to be deeply unsettling. "Inheriting some substantial amount beyond your standard of living is always a profound event," he says. "All of a sudden your menu of choices has been expanded."

At the same time they are dealing with their grief, heirs must make difficult financial and legal decisions. An inheritance can also ignite battles among siblings, upset the balance of power between husband and wife, and send inheritors down a path of destructive behavior.

I've interviewed dozens of financial advisors over the past decade who've said that an inheritance can actually have devastating effects on inheritors. Some lose motivation or quit work, even though their bequest isn't really large enough to make them independently wealthy. "It can be a very crushing blow to people," says certified financial planner J. Steven Cowen. "They're not prepared for how it will change their lives."

Financial planner Henry E. Zapisek recalled the case of a young man who inherited $350,000 a few years ago. He told Zapisek he wanted to invest the money so he could retire early and play golf. Months later, the money was still sitting there. Friends and family gave him advice. "Everyone had a different idea," said Zapisek. "He went into rigor mortis."

Spending Sadly

Some heirs move from paralysis to spending sprees, as if the inheritance were a burden of guilt to be cast off. If they're inexperienced with money, the effect can be disastrous. Virginia Lopez was a nineteen-year-old Southern California student in 1990 when her father died, leaving her $210,000. When she received the first installment of $50,000, she felt wealthy. "It was like, wow, I can go anywhere I want, do anything I want," she told me.

She bought a new truck, ran up charge cards, and didn't keep track of her checking account. Lopez couldn't bear to clear out her father's belongings from his home, which meant she was paying the bills on that unoccupied house as well as on a rental house he had willed her. Within a year, the $50,000 was gone.

Fortunately for Lopez, her grandmother intervened and managed to prevent her receiving more money. Lopez consulted with financial planner Kathryn A. Taylor, who had her take on two jobs to pay the expenses on the houses until they could be sold. Then Taylor showed her how the remaining money if invested could help her reach financial independence at age forty-five. Lopez was grateful to be pulled from the brink. "I won't be doing anything off the wall," she said. "I'll want to, but I know better now."

The Emotional Fallout

Inheritors are often surprised to find that the difficulties they have coping with their windfalls are not unique to

them. Because these difficulties can interfere with successfully managing an inheritance, it's helpful to recognize
them. I've identified the following Six Emotional Stages
of Inheritance. Not everyone will experience these in this
order or experience all of them. And it's common to feel
more than one of these at a time.

1. **Disbelief.** The heir is feeling, "Not this, not now."
Even though we expect our parents to die someday, we
often deny this will really happen to us. Many people
cling to the notion that they are still the children, and not
the adults. So how can they possibly handle all these
grown-up financial issues?

2. **Anger.** In some cases, the adult child thinks, "How
could you die and leave me with such a mess?" Anger can
stem from a sense of abandonment or more concrete
grievances over a parent's failure to leave an orderly estate
or clearly communicate final wishes.

3. **Euphoria.** This is a feeling of "Wow! I've never had
so much money in all my life. Just think of the things I
can do with it: take a vacation, buy a new house, drive a
fancy car, maybe quit work forever." This is when spending starts, and unfortunately, for some people it doesn't
stop until all the money is gone. Some inheritors who
have spent months or years caring for ailing parents jus-
tify it this way: "I've been through hell. I deserve something." So they spend.

4. **Guilt.** These inheritors feel they did nothing to deserve their gifts. They feel they should be enjoying their
bequests, but suffer great guilt that someone had to die

first. Their thinking works like this: "How can I possibly use the money for something fun, like a vacation or new car? How would my parents want me to spend this money? Would they approve?"

5. **Paralysis.** This fear of doing something "wrong" with the money, whether making a poor investment or buying something the benefactor wouldn't have liked, can lead to years of financial stasis. Year in and year out, inheritors leave the assets they've been given sitting untouched exactly where they were at the time of their parents' deaths, from money-market funds and dad's company retirement funds to old family farms.

6. **Heirworthy.** Gradually, over the months and the years, the grief begins to diminish. Inheritors realize that while they can't do all the things they wanted in their euphoric stage, they can still do one or two important ones. And they recognize that while the investments inherited might have been right for mom and dad, they don't necessarily "fit" the younger generation. The parents owned certificates of deposit and utility stocks, but the children need growth investments. The inheritors begin the conversion, usually with the help of an advisor. They also start to appreciate what they've received from their parents and the beneficial changes it can make in their lives. They're learning to preserve it and help it grow, for their own children or for a favorite cause or charity. Now they are no longer passive inheritors, but active money managers.

The Trouble with Affluence

Research has shown that inheritors often feel over-whelmed by what the world views as their good fortune. For their 1988 "Study on Wealth and Philanthropy," Paul G. Schervish and Andrew Herman of the Social Welfare Research Institute at Boston College interviewed 140 wealthy individuals, half of them inheritors, half entre-preneurs. The subjects had either a net worth of at least $1 million or gross income of more than $100,000. Half of them were worth between $5 to $10 million. One of the major revelations of their study, say the authors, was "the experience of wealth as a burden."[1]

Another authoritative study, "Coping with Inherited Wealth" by wealth consultant John L. Levy of Mill Valley, California, first published in 1986, was commissioned by a wealthy man concerned about the effects of his afflu-ence on his children. After interviewing thirty wealthy parents and inheritors, Levy concluded that wealth often made life difficult for inheritors: "Many people who grew up in affluence, knowing that they could expect to re-ceive without effort all that they needed and perhaps con-siderably more, have found that this hasn't been an unmitigated blessing. Too often they are not very happy or fulfilled."[2]

What makes an inheritance potentially burdensome? The size of the bequest, as well as how large it is in rela-tion to the inheritor's current circumstances. Also, the suddenness of the gift and whether it was larger than ex-pected.

For some, problems stem from enforced ignorance

about their wealth. Some inheritors don't know it exists, because the wealth is not discussed and in some cases is even denied or disguised. Schervish and Herman talked to one woman whose father and paternal grandparents denied they owned the bank where her father worked. And even though her father was a banker, she was never taught about money or given an allowance. It was simply never discussed.

"Many people remain virtually in the dark about the monetary value or financial responsibility of their wealth until the day they are to come into their inheritance," the study reports. Several spoke of being sent off to the trust officers at their family's banks when they reached a certain age to be told of their fortunes. One such woman found the experience a substantial shock. "All of a sudden this money is dumped in my lap and everybody goes away and says, 'Good luck.' I was scared to death." She didn't see it as a good thing: "It wasn't, 'oh gee this is great. I'm going to go out and do all this stuff and have a great time.' It was a burden."

In both the Boston College and the Levy studies, the researchers focused mainly on inheritors who received considerable wealth, enough that they didn't have to work. However, their findings about the problems of these inheritors can and often do apply for the merely affluent and the middle class, in other words many of the new inheritance class. Here are some of the major problems identified:

- Low self-worth. Both well-to-do and upper-middle-class inheritors might have had their efforts to achieve self-worth short-circuited when they were young. If their parents' money allowed them to buy their way out of problems, postpone growing up, and avoid the usual bumps and bruises of life that help most people mature, inheritors might never have learned how to persevere or overcome adversity. And without those skills, it's difficult to accomplish most worthwhile things. Achievement and creativity can be dampened by fear of failing, particularly if the parents were highly successful. People who receive a large inheritance may feel, correctly, that the only thing other people notice about them is their money—rather than their skills, interests, or personality. They come to feel that they themselves have no value.

- Conflicted work ethic. Like all of us, inheritors are influenced by certain American notions, that self-reliance and hard work are admirable ethics, that we are all equal and should have equal opportunities, and that we should earn our own way in the world. If inheritors are supported by family wealth and don't need to work, or have only worked for the family business, they could come to believe that they're not capable of supporting themselves. And though they might resent their inheritance at times, they are loath to let it go, fearing they couldn't make it on their own.

- Stigma. Those who are well off sometimes fear being stereotyped as powerful, selfish, exploitative, extravagant, or sheltered. Their affluence tends to spark such negative feelings as envy, anger, and resentment from the world at large. David Bork, founder of the Aspen

Family Business Group in Colorado, once wrote, "It's as if people who have inherited wealth have come to it by some devious or specious method; by accepting the inheritance, they have committed a wrongful deed and are made to feel guilty. The fact is, inheritors are in the 'Lucky Sperm and Egg Club,' a membership over which they have no control."[3]

- Lack of sympathy. Not only are they resented, says Levy, but inheritors have trouble getting a sympathetic hearing for any troubles they may have. "Most Americans," he says, "believe that if they only had enough money and the things it can buy, then they would live in a state of constant bliss." Just like everyone else, inheritors have real problems that require help. But when they seek assistance they might run into the old "if-only-I-had-your-problems" attitude. Some heirs have even found it difficult to find a therapist whose envy of their wealth didn't get in the way.

- Guilt. Inheritors often regret that they have so much, when others have so little. Why were they chosen? "Guilt is the number-one paralyzing issue," says Katherine Gibson, a Virginia inheritor and cofounder of the Inheritance Project, which studies and consults with inheritors. "I cannot tell you how many inheritors I've talked to who feel guilty and ashamed of what they have, that they do nothing constructive with their money." Their sense of unworthiness, says Levy, can run the gamut from being abjectly apologetic all the time to being arrogantly contemptuous.

"The often debilitating degree of guilt that is felt

and expressed by many inheritors is rooted in the fact that they did not earn the freedom and power of wealth through their own creativity or effort," according to the Boston College study. In fact, many participants said they envied those who earned wealth on their own.[4]

Those who receive a large chunk of money are keenly aware that society expects them to be happy. If they instead find it makes them unhappy, they feel even worse, more guilty. Not only didn't they earn this money, they can't even do a good job of enjoying it.

- Too many choices. When money is tight, our choices on how to spend are limited. But when we suddenly have more of it, the choices can be overwhelming. A sports car or a new house, an index fund or a hedge fund, a European vacation or a private boarding school? "A plentitude of options can be paralyzing," says Levy, "and can make it very difficult to develop the capacity to make sensible and intelligent decisions."

- Isolation. This problem, says Stolper, is also known as "the tall poppy—you've risen above your class. You lose friends, not because of anything you do." One fifty-year-old woman of modest means who inherited $200,000 from her father, feared being ostracized by friends when a stepsister began discussing the inheritance at the woman's hair salon. "People believe I'm well off," the woman recalls. "Someone said, 'I understand you're a millionaire.' It just dropped my stomach out."

- Solicitations. Inheritors are often seen by others as cash cows for loans, gifts, and contributions. And many heirs succumb. "There is guilt associated with inheritance," says Stolper. "One way of doing penance is to give it away." Friends and relatives who ask for money really believe that if they were in your shoes, they'd be generous, says Stolper. It's a way to take the moral high ground.

- Suspiciousness. People of means often regard others warily, and with good reason. "Many of those they encounter," says Levy, "want something from the affluent person and are ready to manipulate or use him or her for their own purposes." Unfortunately, having such experiences leads to what Levy describes as one of the most painful and damaging aspects of inheritance, difficulty believing that people like them for themselves. That, in turn, makes it hard to form good relationships.

- Family expectations. In families with a tradition of affluence and success, parents often raise their children to meet high expectations or even carry on a dynasty of sorts. While some children thrive under these demands, others find them a burden or a hindrance. It is a challenge for adult children in these families to carve out their own identities, separate from their parents'.

JUDGE NOT

WHEN RESEARCHERS SCHERVISH and Herman set out to study the experience and beliefs of the wealthy, they expected to meet resistance from their subjects on these normally taboo topics: "For many of the wealthy, particularly those who have inherited, talking about money even to friends and family is considered to be something akin to what one respondent described as 'speaking publicly about rape and death.'" But as it turned out, the subjects were quite willing to talk and were candid in their answers. In fact, most enjoyed the experience. The researchers attributed the cooperation to the "simple therapeutic value of being closely questioned and listened to by someone who was sincerely and unjudgmentally interested in what was being said."

My "Tall Poppy" Tales

When we moved from our first home into our dream home, I naively expected everyone I knew to share in our happiness. Although we could have purchased the larger home without the inheritance, it would have been a challenge: Using some of the inheritance for part of the down payment provided a cushion. So I was unprepared for the cold water thrown on my enthusiasm. I'd been to the house before, which was owned by the family of a technology company executive, and heard people exclaiming how lovely it was. When I told some of these same people that my family was moving in, what I heard instead was, "Oh, I wouldn't want that house, too much to clean." Another acquaintance said, "But there aren't any children in that neighborhood." (Not true, it turned out. I later saw her son playing with one of the nonexistent children.) I soon learned to recognize these spontaneous remarks as a way for people to enumerate out loud the reasons why they really don't envy your good fortune.

One poor woman who'd just learned where I was moving let her jaw drop open, then said, "Who died and left you money?" She was quickly hustled aside and told just *who* had died, and was profusely apologetic. After we'd moved in, a friend of my husband's who runs his own business looked around the bedroom I'd converted to my workplace and said with disbelief, "Your office is bigger than mine." Sometimes people simply say nothing, as if withholding approval. Call it envy or resentment, there's sometimes a chilly level of discomfort and disapproval that we haven't stayed in our place. While those who earn their wealth can be subject to the "tall poppy" syndrome also, the world seems inclined to be more admiring and cut them a bit of slack.

Some wealthy people hide out by taking up occupations and lifestyles of the upper middle class, and don't use the money for consumption. Others simply adapt to their surroundings. Financial planner Myra Salzer told the *Journal of Financial Planning* about a young man who liked to play basketball, but the games were held on the other side of town with players of very modest means. So when he drove there three times a week, he took what he called his "basketball car," an old Chevy with paint on the bumper, so he could blend in as just one of the guys.

Of course, that doesn't solve the everyday challenges of coping with an inheritance. Some heirs find help through a support group. Joan Cudhea, an inheritor and a certified financial planner, belongs to a wealth support group of ten women. Many were poor or middle class when they were younger. They discuss what kind of cars to drive, how to deal with old friends, and how to pass good values on to their children. "It is one of the very few places," says Cudhea, "you can feel safe to say you have issues about wealth."

Chapter 7

From the Grave

Things have a terrible permanence when people die.
—Joyce Kilmer

When Vicky's father died, she and her brother inherited his most prized possession, the furniture store he'd run in a poor part of town. The store did well when her father was alive, but gradually competition from national chains put a squeeze on profits. Vicky and her brother, who had successful careers separate from the store, are the owners and landlords. After more than twenty years, the two heirs no longer receive rent or profits from the business. In fact, they contribute thousands of dollars annually to keep it running.

"That store is very important to my brother and me," says Vicky. "It is very symbolic." Her father was proud that the store paid for Vicky's college education at a top private college. Vicky, for her part, is proud that her father opened the store in the barrio and that he gave credit to people who couldn't otherwise pay. Her father picked out his gravesite on a cemetery hill that looks across a valley to a certain tall building. Says Vicky: "He wanted, from his grave, to see the store."

Like Vicky and her brother, inheritors often regard what they've received as more than assets. A family business isn't just a shop, but the embodiment of a parent. Keeping it going is a kind of memorial. A stock isn't just another investment. It represents Dad and the savvy investor he was, or Mom and the company where she worked for twenty-five years. Holding on to it is like being wrapped in a security blanket. A house is not a piece of real estate, but the family homestead, where collective memory resides. Retaining it is a way to keep the past alive. When passed from one person to another through inheritance, assets can be imbued with profound meaning. Some financial advisors call it the "heirloom effect."

One woman told me that she and her two sisters kept her father's wallet with his credit cards and $38 in it in a lock box for two years after his death. Though they had inherited hundreds of thousands of dollars from him they felt reticent about removing the money from his wallet and pocketing it. It wasn't just another handful of cash. Because it had been in his wallet it was far more personal. They finally resolved the problem by using the money to go out to dinner together.

Many inheritors cling to investments or property they receive—even when it doesn't make good financial or common sense. They will hang on to large blocks of one stock or to expensive property that they would otherwise never dream of going out and buying. These inheritors often acknowledge that their behavior is illogical and potentially harmful to their long-term security. But their need to preserve a connection to the loved one comes first.

A successful health-care manager named Pam has wrestled for years with her inability to use the money her parents left her. "The overwhelming feeling I've had is I don't want to spend the money," she says. "If I spent that, my parents were really gone."

Inheritors like Pam often don't want to change how their money is invested because they don't want to separate from the loved ones who left it to them. Psychologist Olivia Mellan counsels financial advisors that when it comes to inheritors they must learn patience: "If you don't make a little space for their fears and anxieties, they'll bolt from your office and never take your advice."

Stuck on a Stock

This is not at all unusual, says Dan Moisand, a certified financial planner in Melbourne, Florida. "It is common for people to inherit assets and set those assets aside as if they were an urn," he says. One client he advised had inherited stock in the company where her late father had worked. Moisand worried that the stock represented too big a portion of her assets and advised her to diversify to lower her risk. But she was reluctant, saying her father must have kept it "for a reason." Moisand finally succeeded, after persuading her the money could jump-start college funds for her children—and that her father would have approved.

Getting inheritors to divest an inherited stock holding can be a challenge, many financial advisors agree. "It's almost like cutting an umbilical cord," says Rene de Charon, a California certified financial planner. The task can be doubly hard if the stock has been a star performer for many years. CPA Richard J. Muscio recalls one client who inherited a big chunk of American Express stock, his parents' one big winning investment. The client was loath to sell and go against his parents, says Muscio, because "for forty years that's all they ever talked about."

THE RISK IN LOYALTY

WHAT'S WRONG WITH owning one stock? You're putting your financial security at high risk. "Anything bad can happen to just one stock," says Craig J. Hillegas, a certified financial planner in Escondido, California. The stock market might plummet by 30 percent in one year, but it eventually rebounds. But the stock of one company can go to zero and never recover. That's why investment experts recommend that a portfolio of individual stocks should have at least fifteen to twenty diverse stocks. It's also why many advisors recommend mutual funds, which contain hundreds of stocks, to spread the risk even more.

Even the best blue-chip stocks can stumble and fall. Consider these market heavyweights: Procter & Gamble, McDonald's Corporation, Gillette Co., Coca-Cola, and IBM. At some point in the past thirty years, each has plunged by more than 50 percent. When Procter & Gamble fell from $117

to $55 in early 2000, employees and retirees who had
stocked up on the company shares had to revise their financial plans. Many blue-chip companies make a comeback.
Some, such as Woolworth and Polaroid, never do.

Wendy, a Los Angeles print-shop employee, came
from a family that had also enjoyed the fruits of a one-
stock wonder I'll call the DBP (Dull But Profitable)
Corp. When her father, a writer, died, she inherited almost $200,000 worth of DBP. Within several years its
worth had risen to $600,000. At first she was paralyzed.
"It was three years before I could do anything with it,"
she says. "It was sitting there gathering dividends."
Eventually she spent some of the dividends and cashed
out some shares to buy a car, fund an IRA, and fix up her
condo. Nine years later, it is by far her biggest single asset. She knows she should diversify, but selling is not an
option she will consider.

In fact, she's even bought more shares at times, to get
back to the same number of shares her father left her. "I
don't want to lose a penny he gave me," she says. "I just
don't feel worthy. This was a gift. I didn't do anything
here."

Father Knows Best

This sense of unworthiness is one I've encountered repeatedly with inheritors. Clearly, guilt over receiving
money as a result of a loved one's death and guilt at not
having earned it are at work here. But in some cases, like

the next example, there's something I call the "eulogy effect," the tendency to idealize the benefactor as having special wisdom and infallibility while minimizing the inheritor's own abilities.

A few years ago I ran into a friend named Laurie, who was attending an investment conference where I was speaking. She told me that her father, a retired businessman who invested successfully in the stock market as a hobby, had died a few months earlier, leaving her a $200,000 stock portfolio. That day she was doing her best to take a crash course in investing to better learn how to manage the bequest, but felt she would never be as competent as her father.

In his final years, she recalled, her father spent hours before the television, avidly watching the stock quotes roll by on CNBC. He kept the sound on the TV down while he listened to classical music and wouldn't let anyone change the channel. He read *The Wall Street Journal* every day. The stocks he'd chosen had done well during the bull market of the late 1990s, but after he died, their value began to drop. Laurie felt this was somehow her fault and that she'd let her dad down. I told her that the entire stock market had fallen and she shouldn't take the blame. But she reiterated sadly that she could never do as well as he did: "My dad always made the right decisions."

Neil Hokanson, an investment manager in Solana Beach, California, says inheritors who idealize a parent's investment track record probably haven't done an impartial review. Nonetheless, they try to guide their financial lives by parental words of wisdom. Then it falls to an investment advisor to gently chip away at the statements made by Mom or Dad that the inheritors regard as chiseled in stone.

One of Hokanson's clients who inherited money from her father told him: "Dad said never sell a drug company stock." The problem with these pronouncements, says Hokanson, is that circumstances could always trump them: The human genome project could set the drug industry on its ear, for example, or the nationalization of prescription drug delivery could decimate profits. Hokanson ultimately talked the woman into reducing her pharmaceutical holdings, but only somewhat. One widow, whose entire net worth was invested in a defense company where her husband worked, didn't heed his advice. She found another advisor, who didn't persuade her to diversify. She subsequently lost millions.

Financial advisors must carefully weigh an inheritor's emotions with what they see as their responsibility to protect their clients from excessive risk. It's a delicate balance between nudging and waiting for signs the clients are ready to think about the future. As a way to prod them into diversifying, Hokanson asks heirs whether they would want to leave their own children with an investment legacy that ties their hands. "Look forward," he urges them, "not backward."

John Nofsinger, a finance professor at Washington State University in Pullman, Washington, and author of a behavioral finance book called *Investment Madness: How Psychology Affects Your Investing . . . and What To Do About*

It, says that inheritors (and their advisors) should strive to make a mental shift. Inheritors shouldn't focus on a parent's decision to own or hold on to an asset, but on the parent's decision to leave it to them. That, says Nofsinger, leads to a more reasonable outlook: "Dad's wish isn't for me to hold this stock. What Dad wants is for me to be financially secure."

That approach is what finally worked for a woman named Peggy. A lively, charismatic music teacher, Peggy admired her father's skill at managing money and investing, but felt she had no aptitude for them. When she inherited part of his stock holdings after his death, she wanted to preserve them.

"For the longest time I wouldn't sell. The thought of selling made my heart beat fast. I felt that my dad would disapprove," she recalls. Instead of selling, when she wanted to use the money, she borrowed on margin from the brokerage firm and paid interest. But when the stock market fell, she had to make good on the loan by selling some of her holdings. Finally, an investment advisor counseled her not to continue borrowing on margin, saying, "Your father would hate that." So Peggy sold the stocks, met with the advisor, and developed a plan. But Peggy regrets how she handled the inheritance: "At first I felt like I was letting my father down. Where I failed my father was in not appreciating the gift enough to protect it enough in its original form. I wasn't as good a steward as I could or should have been."

Still Seeking Parental Approval

In some cases, a forceful parent with strong ideas about money can leave heirs in crisis. Consider the young woman who inherited $80,000 from her father, a Midwestern farmer. He viewed land as good and desirable, but thought of money as sinful. Although the woman wanted to invest her bequest, for more than two years she left it untouched in a money-market fund. Selling what her father valued (the farm) and turning it into what he despised (cash) left her conflicted.

One interior designer I know used some of the money she received from her parents to buy a house. Then she went out and bought some original artwork to hang in the house, but didn't put it up. The art sat wrapped in paper in a closet. Why? Because her parents would find the purchase frivolous, she told me. Buying a house was practical, but the artwork was not. A psychiatrist to whom I told this anecdote said that even something negative like disapproval can in a strange way help preserve the connection to the loved one.

When her parents died, Amy, an only child, received half their estate for herself and the other half to manage for her two children. She wanted to use some of her money to make a real estate investment, but found herself frozen with dread. "My dad was a saver," she says. "He hoarded it while he was alive." She worried about making a mistake or using it in way Father wouldn't approve. "I feel like I have to ask permission of someone. God, if I spend this, my dad will be flipping over in his grave. He never did anything risky."

When a House Will Always Be Home

Selling the family home can be traumatic, and many heirs tend to postpone it. Unfortunately, a home is often one of the largest assets in an estate—and one of the most expensive to maintain. Even if the mortgage is paid off, other expenses such as property tax, insurance, water, and electricity must be paid, whether or not the house is occupied.

After his dad died, Wes and his brother were left with the family home in an older area near Chicago. His brother wanted to keep it and rent it, but Wes did not. So his brother bought out his half. For years the brother lovingly played the role of landlord, driving five hours roundtrip on the weekends to garden or fix the screens. "It was part of the grieving process," Wes says. Wes advised him to sell and buy elsewhere, noting that the home was appreciating only modestly. Finally, after six years, the brother did. "It had been long enough," says Wes. "The house was just a house."

I found selling the home where I grew up an emotionally wrenching experience. Because I was an only child and had moved away from my hometown, selling the house was like finally saying good-bye to my parents and my childhood. I put it off for more than a year, making occasional trips to check up on the property. It was after my return from one of these visits that I realized it was time to sell. I was showing some photos of the house to a friend, trying to explain how special the house was, how the afternoon sun came in through the dining room windows in the winter. But when I viewed the photos through her eyes, I could see an old house that looked dusty and faded from neglect. It was slowly deteriorating. The house where I grew up no longer existed, except in my head.

When the time came to sell his parents' house, my husband did not hesitate, though he allowed himself one bit of sentimentality. We had joked affectionately that the house was a fifties museum, only 1,100 square feet, never remodeled, dwarfed by a giant fir in the front yard. It was furnished with maple and the cozy kitchen still had a Formica-top table with matching metal chairs.

When the escrow agent asked my husband to come by his office and sign the paperwork, my husband said no. I'm going to sign it at the kitchen table at the house. The agent tried to explain that it wasn't done that way. My husband held firm. In the end, my husband signed while sitting at the Formica table. When the check for his half of the proceeds came, he simply signed it and gave it to me, as the family money manager. He doesn't ask much about it. Nor has he looked through the boxes of memorabilia from the house that his brother thoughtfully packed and mailed. He just went back to work.

The Kodachrome Home

In addition to deciding what to do with the family home, some heirs are also faced with the tough choice of whether to keep the family vacation home by the beach or in the mountains. Financial planner Moisand describes the downside of retaining the vacation home: the grown children feel obligated to keep the cabin because Mom and Dad wanted them to. But it's hard for some of the offspring to support and even harder for others to travel across country to enjoy it. "They have so many memories of vacations in the mountains," he says. "But it wears thin. It changes the experience of the home. They have to haul themselves up there to do maintenance. It's difficult to do it 600 miles away." (Moisand suggests that parents who want their children to continue enjoying the home consider earmarking money from the estate just for maintenance.)

Here are my reasons for keeping my family's summer home, all of them emotional. But first the bad news. Our 1913 summer cottage on Lake Michigan sits on a tall sand dune overlooking the lake. Because of high water and erosion, the house was moved back away from the lake and toward the road in the 1970s. Now we have nowhere left to move. The water has been low, fortunately, but that could change. The home's wooden exterior has withstood decades of sun and snow, but now must be replaced at a cost of thousands of dollars. It's not insulated, so we can't rent it out except a few weeks in the summer when we like to be there. We have to fly several thousand miles to get there, so zipping up for the weekend is out of the question. While the property is appreciating (even as the cliff gradually crumbles into the lake), only time will tell whether we would have been better off financially selling and investing the money.

But it nevertheless seems like a slice of heaven to my

family. I've known the families who own the surrounding Dunewood cottages all my life, so it's like going home. In the majority of cases, the grown children who've inherited cottages from their parents have kept them and some even travel as far as we do to get there. My children enjoy the sense of heritage and traditions built up over the years. However, they and my husband sometimes complain, with good reason, that going to Michigan leaves us without the time or money to vacation elsewhere. Of course, we could always sell it. But I would give it long and hard consideration first—I've seen far too many people, when I mention our cottage, get misty-eyed over the summer home that someone in their family let slip away.

Mixed feelings seem to rule the day when families decide to keep inherited vacation homes. One New Yorker and mother of a toddler says that she and her three siblings begin to argue about how to share their 800-square-foot Long Island summer cottage every year as Memorial Day rolls around. All four siblings and their families want to stay almost every weekend. "It is a terrible source of conflict, always tears shed," she says, "but no one could bear to let it go, so we work something out and smooth things over just enough to make it until Labor Day!"

GO FISH OR GO WITHOUT

ONE OF THE things I inherited was the rights to the card game my paternal grandmother developed, the first mass-marketed children's game of Go Fish. I also inherited a desire to keep the game—and the royalties—going. When crayon maker Binney & Smith discontinued marketing the game in 1987, I was crushed that this bit of family heritage was no more. I had the presence of mind to ensure the rights were legally mine by hiring a lawyer to tie up loose ends on the marketing agreement. Then I made a few feeble attempts to market the game to other distributors. I had some serious nibbles, but no bites. If felt that if I could just get the game out on the market and show a favorable sales record, it could be revived. At one point I even employed the services of business students at a local university who came up with ideas as a marketing class project.

But I began to realize how much time, energy, and money it could take. Did I really want to spend more than $15,000 printing a first run of the game and turn my living room into a Go Fish distribution center? I was already busy with two young children and my own writing career. I'd go back and forth, one day thinking I couldn't let my family down, the other admitting that I just couldn't handle such a big project. Finally, a friend helped me see my dilemma more clearly. "Creating children's games was your grandmother's dream," she told me. "Writing books is yours." I had to agree, but I never stopped wishing I could keep the game alive. Little did I know my early efforts might eventually pay off. (See Chapter 15, Heirworthy.)

Of course, not all inheritances that come with emotional baggage cause stress or discomfort. Sometimes the baggage contains good things. One friend of mine received a $5,000 bequest from a great aunt of whom she was fond. She happily used it to take a trip, feeling that it was an appropriate way to honor her aunt's memory.

And despite the stress her inheritance sometimes causes her, Wendy, who worries about owning $600,000 in just one stock, is still relieved to have it. "Without the inheritance, I'd be working until I was seventy-five. Now I know I will be able to retire. Dad has left me in a good position," she says. She feels grateful she can lead a middle-class life. "I can still go to dinner with the girls. It is a fantastic gift. I thank my father every day."

Chapter 8

Yours, Mine, or Ours?

I, John, take thee, Jane, to my wedded wife, to have and
to hold from this day forward, for better for worse,
for richer for poorer . . .
—Wedding Vows, Book of Common Prayer

If you took these vows when you married, you probably thought that of the two alternatives, poorer was the worse. But what happens if, thanks to an inheritance, one of you is already richer before you step up to the altar? Or, more likely, what if one of you becomes an inheritor during the marriage? As the number of inheritors grows steadily, more couples must grapple with this question: Will the inheritance be yours, mine, or ours?

Many people assume, particularly if they live in a community property state, that an inheritance received by one spouse is automatically the property of both. The misunderstanding is a common one, says attorney Russell Griffith. In fact, he says, "Anything that's a gift or an inheritance is separate property." If the inheriting spouse decides to keep the property separate, this can cause considerable hurt feelings and strain for an otherwise happily married couple. It's like introducing a prenuptial agreement—years after the marriage. And prenups aren't popular with most couples before they walk down the aisle.

Yet financial and legal advisors often recommend that clients who have received an inheritance before they wed opt for a premarital agreement. The advisors point out that keeping assets separate is the cleanest method in the event of a divorce and that these agreements help prevent the noninheritor spouse from taking advantage of the one with the inherited money. (Keep in mind, though, that advisors have to err on the side of caution to protect their clients and themselves lest they be sued for failing to help inheritors preserve their fortunes.) Unfortunately, a premarital agreement can have a chilling effect on a relationship—particularly if it is foisted on a prospective spouse by the wealthy family of the inheritor. After all, no matter how you cut it, a premarital agreement is essentially a will for the death of the marriage.

Let's say that Steve, who is twenty-five, has received $750,000 from his late grandmother. His family is urging him to keep it separate property when he marries Lisa, also twenty-five and without any assets of her own, knowing that a divorce could cost him half of his inheritance. Whether or not the couple signs a prenuptial, it is essential that the couple talk and reach some agreement before the marriage, says John L. Levy, the Mill Valley wealth consultant. "A central element in every good marriage is open discussion of all issues, and most especially those involving money," he says.

Society can still be harsh on couples if the woman has considerably more money than the man, says Levy. Men can be viewed as lazy or parasitic, and their self-images can suffer. So while affluent men are seen as desirable marital prospects, affluent women struggle to find suitable mates. "When should I tell the person I'm dating that I'm wealthy? How much do I share?" These are the kinds of questions that Valerie Jacobs, San Diego psychologist and wealth consultant, hears from young heiresses. Jacobs, herself an inheritor to a fortune, says that she's seen women get divorced as many as four times because their spouses couldn't handle the disparity in wealth. "Men tend to equate money with success," says Jacobs. She knows of one woman who inherited millions from her family, but lives on her husband's income. The woman signed over the house to her husband, so if they ever got a divorce he would have a valuable asset.

Clearly, couples in which the wife has the most valuable assets must work at communicating and sharing. If the husband is supported solely by the wife, he can feel ashamed and guilty. The wife, on the other hand, could feel suspicious or even contemptuous, says Levy. That's why he believes it's critical for the wife to respect the husband's vocation, whether he works for a paycheck, manages her money, or does philanthropic work. "Without this kind of respect, the couple haven't much of a chance," he says. Levy offers three principles for such marriages: discuss promptly and openly all issues, encourage parents to accept the couple as autonomous adults, and find shared interests and commitments.

But what if the inheritance arrives after the marriage? "It can represent a complete shift of power in the household, particularly if the heir was not the main breadwinner," says San Diego financial advisor Michael Stolper. If the wife is the inheritor, says Stolper, and the bequest is all that she owns by herself, her message to her husband could be: "Keep your hands off my money." She could be highly protective of it, because it represents power and independence.

"It can be a very disconcerting event. There can be a lot of strain and conflict," says attorney Mary Clarno. If the heir decides to keep the money separate, the noninheriting spouse could be left feeling hurt: What about me? How could you do that? While many people are uncomfortable with the idea of having separate property, that's usually how they proceed, says Clarno. Typical reasons include honoring the wishes of the giver, wanting to keep the gift within the family, and desiring to preserve assets for children.

There are other legitimate reasons to keep inherited money separate. If you convert your inheritance to community property, you could be setting up some negative consequences for your family in the event of the two dreaded Big Ds: your death before your spouse's or a divorce. Should you die first, some or all of your inheritance could end up in the possession of your spouse's next partner and not with your children, as you would prefer.

(You can try to protect against this through estate planning, however.)

In the case of divorce, you could well regret your generous decision years earlier to share your inheritance with your spouse. Then your options during divorce proceedings are to allow your estranged spouse to take a large portion of it or to spend thousands of dollars having a forensic accountant trace your money back to its origins. Things can get sticky. For example, if a wife makes the down payment on a home with her separate money, but the husband makes most of the mortgage payments, to whom does the appreciation belong in the event of divorce? It depends on the circumstances and the laws of the state in which they live.

Property owned before marriage and gifts and inheritance received are considered separate property. But commingling what was once separate property with community property doesn't mean it's gone forever, says Ginita Wall, a California forensic accountant who specializes in divorce. "If you can trace it, you can get it back," she says. "It just means you've got some work to do, or your accountant has some work to do." In one divorce case where her client kept good financial records, Wall was able to trace the woman's separate property back twenty-six years.

Rebecca, a woman in her fifties with a longtime live-in boyfriend, has kept her inheritance separate but feels pangs of guilt: "You feel like the right thing is to share it." Inheritors are clearly susceptible to this thinking. Jacobs knows of one woman whose husband kept his inheritance separate until he couldn't stand to hear his wife nag him every time they had to buy something by saying, "It's your money. It's your decision." He finally gave her half.

For others, having a spouse keep property separate is not a deal-breaker in the marriage. Financial advisor Candace Bahr recalls one woman who received an inheritance decades before and kept it as separate property from her husband's. She held on to it when they divorced and continued to keep it separate years later when they married for the second time.

One married woman with a young child keeps most of her inheritance separate, though she knows her father would have hated the practice. Her husband, however, is happy for her to feel as if she has a safety net, no doubt she says, because his own mother is divorced and struggling with money.

Jean Sinclair, a certified financial planner, recalls one stay-at-home mother of five who inherited $1 million from her mother. She opted to keep the money separate but spent freely on her children and husband. The separate account dismayed her husband, the family breadwinner. "He didn't really think it was fair," Sinclair says. "He felt, 'I'm working—everything I'm earning is going to the family.'" Sinclair encouraged him to think of the money more as an heirloom, or personal property, than simply cash.

In one case an advisor shared with me, the inheritor never gave her spouse a chance to react—she simply kept it a big secret from him. The wife was a flight attendant who received a bequest of $750,000 that included a condominium in another city. She simply had all mail relating to the inheritance and the condo sent there and because she was often out of town, her absence wasn't unusual.

A Tale of Two Spouses

Even when husband and wife tackle these issues head-on, the feelings of hurt and worry don't necessarily go away. Here's a case in point. When Nancy, a San Francisco businesswoman in her forties, received a $250,000 inheritance from her father, she was predisposed to keep it separate from her husband, Jim, a resort manager.

It wasn't that their marriage was shaky. It was that both she and Jim had come from divorced families. She didn't have a happily-ever-after view of marriage. She remembers what it was like when her own parents divorced, and how her mother had no way to earn a living and no credit cards in her name. Nancy liked the idea of keeping separate accounts. During the time she and Jim lived together before getting married, each kept his or her own checking account.

When she got the inheritance, Nancy consulted an attorney and asked if the money was legally her separate property. He told her it was, but that "a great inequity was going to be created." It wasn't the size of the inheritance itself, he said, but how her husband was likely to view her treatment of it.

He urged her to give some of the money outright to

her husband immediately. The attorney suggested paying off his car and student loans, which Nancy did. He also recommended investing in Jim's "earning power," such as funding an advanced degree. (As it turned out Jim was climbing his career ladder quite well without it.) Nancy also set aside a portion of the bequest in a joint account. To help reduce the disparity in their retirement savings, Nancy agreed to pay more of the bills (although she earned less), so Jim could funnel more of his salary into his 401(k).

Someday, Nancy will receive an inheritance from her mother, which she plans to handle the same way. She says that her husband was understandably alarmed when she consulted an attorney about the first bequest because "it almost implies distrust. It increases tension. The inescapable conclusion is that you want it . . . just in case."

Over the years, she felt more and more comfortable spending that money, to help with the down payment on a new home and buying a car. She feels that she and Jim have reached a certain comfort level with the inheritance.

But when she invited him to share his feelings with me and with her, Jim painted a much different picture. Although Nancy reassures him that she's not planning for a divorce, he says he can't help but think: "So it's separate for what reason?" When she decided to keep the inheritance in her name only, he recalls feeling that suddenly their joint retirement goals weren't a concern anymore. She was taken care of, but he would have to work harder to make his.

"We never did resolve it," says Jim. "We've survived mostly by ignoring the issue. We don't think about it. We don't talk about it."

Jim came from a large family of modest means. He recalled an important milestone in his financial life: Living paycheck to paycheck after college and carrying five student loans left him with a bad feeling. When he finally managed to accumulate $500 in savings, it changed his outlook and he felt great relief. "Your whole perspective on life changes when there's a cushion," he says. But Nancy's cushion isn't his, he says, it's hers. "You still feel the big gap?" Nancy asks. "Sure," he says. "It changes everyone's life to have it parked there."

The Benefits of Sharing

While many financial and legal advisors recommend keeping inherited assets as separate property, there are financial benefits to making them community property, says estate planning attorney James D. Miller. Two of them involve estate planning. The first deals with the estate tax and the second with taxes on capital gains.

Here's a simplified version example of the first reason. Let's assume the husband is worth $1.8 million, his wife has $200,000, and the tax law allows individuals to pass on $1 million each to beneficiaries free of estate taxes. If the husband dies first and leaves his $1.8 million to his wife (spouses can leave unlimited amounts to each other free of estate tax), she can pass along only $1 million of her $2 million to her heirs without generating estate taxes. About half of the second $1 million could be lost to taxes. The couple has not been able to maximize their potential unified estate tax credit (available to married couples who do certain estate planning) that would allow them to pass $2 million free of estate taxes to their beneficiaries.

Here's the other kind of tax problem that can be prevented if assets are combined rather than kept separate in marriage. All property and investments have a "basis," or value for the purposes of determining the taxes paid on profits or capital gains taxes. In the case of stock, the basis can be the purchase price. But if the stockholder dies, there is what's known as a "step-up in basis," to the value of the stock at the owner's death, say from $100,000 to $500,000. This can be a valuable increase if it saves an inheritor from paying capital gains taxes of, let's say, 20 percent on $400,000, or $80,000.

If the spouse who has few assets dies first, the survivor will get little or no benefit from the rules on basis. But if the wealthier spouse had given half his stock to his wife, as a widower he would get a tax break when inheriting the stock and receiving a step-up in basis. In community property states, says Miller, there's an added incentive for married inheritors to share. Assets held as community property get a full step-up in basis, not a partial increase. So both the wife's and the husband's share of the stock investment would get a step up.

Think It Over

As must be obvious, these issues can be highly complex and should be well thought out. Tax laws are constantly changing. Before sharing your inheritance, says Miller, "You would certainly want to make sure you were in a stable marriage." He adds that you should also take an affirmative step (signing legal legal documents that vary by state) to verify that you are sharing or giving away property when you commingle assets.

Griffith says that many couples are understandably reluctant to grapple with these thorny issues. "They don't think about problems with their spouse down the road," he says. "That's the natural reaction of people who are married and love each other. Divorce and death are the last things on their mind." But given that we all die and that the divorce rate remains at 50 percent, even happily married couples need to discuss just who owns what and how they want their assets distributed when they die.

Many couples don't give these property ownership issues much thought—until one spouse receives an inheritance. That prompts them to assume, correctly, that they need to speak with an attorney about their own estate plans. But they can be stunned to learn that the inheriting spouse should make a choice about whether to share the bequest before estate planning can be completed.

That's when we learned that I had to make a choice. For me the issues boiled down to: Would I feel worried and insecure about the possibility of divorce if the inheritance were shared? (No.) Would I feel better knowing there would be more money for my two sons to inherit if I shared the assets? (Yes.) Also, the issue of separateness just didn't sit right with me emotionally, although I knew it was sensible to consider. In the years since I signed a document acknowledging that I was sharing my inheritance, circumstances have altered. Changes in the tax law that could eventually eliminate the estate tax would also remove one incentive I had to share my inheritance. On the other hand, my husband's subsequent inheritance, which he readily shared with me, has made our finances seem more evenly balanced.

Olivia Mellan, psychologist and author, says that if one spouse chooses to keep an inheritance separate it raises issues of control and distrust. The noninheriting partner wonders: Why do you want separate money? The heir asks: Why do you want my money? "It's all so emotionally loaded," Mellan says. "These are very core issues. You have to discuss it. Money is never just money."

There are no right answers in these situations, says Mellan. But in every marriage there should be a mix of communal money and autonomous money for each partner. Her advice to couples when one gets an inheritance: communicate, communicate, communicate. And don't negotiate a financial resolution until all feelings are fully aired.

All in the Family

Say not you know another entirely, till
you have divided an inheritance with
him.—*Johann Kaspar Zavater*

If siblings fight over their parents' estates, it's little wonder. They've been fighting with one another for years over whatever resources their parents had to offer. "Usually it's more than just the immediate financial issues," says Shirley Kovar, estate planning attorney and mediator. "It's 'Mom liked you more than she liked me.'" Mellan says that often when siblings fight in such circumstances, "You're very much talking about who was the favorite child."

One woman I know lovingly took care of her mother in the months before the elder woman died. She expected only a modest inheritance at best. What she got instead was a nasty shock. Only after her mother's death did the woman learn that her mother had already given her home to the woman's charming but irresponsible younger sister. It wasn't the gift itself that upset her, but the secret between her mother and sister. Despite the younger sister's pleas, the woman didn't speak to her for more than ten years.

In situations like these, the adult child is angry with the parent, but takes these feelings out on the person who seems to be the real source of the problem—the sibling. It's too painful to admit anger or disappointment with the parent (we don't speak ill of the dead, plus we are probably too heartbroken). It's not so much about the inheritance. It's what the inheritance says about Mom and Dad's feelings for us.

Sometimes parents favor one child who is perceived as weaker or needier than their other children. Jacobs says parents are often tempted to do this because "it's hard not to rescue someone who's in trouble." But in the eyes of siblings who get less, it could be the final example of the parents' lifelong coddling of that one child. For once, why couldn't it just be equal?

If children feel strongly about favoritism, it can be helpful for them to talk with their parents before it's too late. Jacobs recalls the case of a woman who was married to a successful man. Her brothers, however, could not keep a job and lived off handouts from their prosperous parents. Even though she led a comfortable life, the woman was bothered by the fact that she had gotten nothing from her parents. Finally she told her parents how she felt. They sympathized and gave her a gift of money. Having her parents listen and respond made the woman feel much better.

Some parents give money to their children on what they see as an "as needed" basis. This can include college tuition, a first car, or help with a down payment on a house. If the parents help underwrite the daughter who went to medical school, but expend no money for the computer geek son who founded his own company at twenty, is that fair? Should the parents make it up to him in their estate? And later in life, should parents grant more to the sibling who does most of the caregiving? Parents can alleviate some of the stress surrounding these real and perceived inequities by talking about their philosophy of giving to their children and by spelling out their plans for their bequests.

While sibling rivalries can be intense when settling a parent's estate, the fact is that most brothers and sisters manage to get along and come to an accommodation. One woman, knowing her brother liked her father's resort condominium, suggested he buy it at a discount from her and the other siblings.

Even bad behavior is not enough to break the bond between many siblings. One woman told me that soon after her mother died, her sister surreptitiously took what she wanted from the mother's house, packed it in the mother's Volkswagen, and drove away. When I asked if they were still close, the woman shrugged her shoulders and said, "What could I do? She's my sister." One man was troubled to find, after his parents died, that his younger brother had taken the set of family wine glasses without any discussion. The older brother had been in the habit of opening wine and serving at every family occasion. He was upset, but had decided to let it pass. After all, he said, "He's my brother."

The loss of both parents, according to Victoria Secunda's *Losing Your Parents, Finding Your Self,* often marks a change in the sibling relationship. In her survey, 76 percent of adult orphans found their feelings for their siblings had changed. Of those who cited a change, one-third had become more distant, but two-thirds said they had grown closer.

For some, it was the time spent working together to care for the parent and arranging the funeral that brought them closer. "In many cases," writes Secunda, "the parents had been an emotional 'wedge' between siblings by displaying obvious favoritism; with this barrier gone, the siblings were able to rediscover, even discover, one another." Secunda found that only a minority of adult children who received less of an inheritance than their siblings nursed a grudge about it.

Parents can leave estate plans that set children at one another's throats or that strengthen their bonds. Charles Foster II, a certified financial planner, tells of one very large estate that the parents divided into four shares—one for each of their three children and one for a charitable family foundation. "The foundation," says Foster, "helped bring them closer together."

Chapter 9

Get Real

Dollars do better if they are accompanied by sense.
—Earl Riney

Whether your inheritance is $5,000 or $5 million, you've probably fantasized about the many ways you could use that money. Depending on your current standard of living and the size of your bequest, the list of possibilities running through your head can go on and on: take a trip, buy a car, pay for a child's college education, buy a house, change careers, start a business, pay off debt, save for retirement, and still have money left over for charity. Inheritors can seem a bit frenetic as they think out loud about what they'll do. They seem to be trying on new ideas like clothes in a store, to see which one fits. They can also go a bit wild.

A writer I know in New Jersey shared a good-sized estate from his great-uncle with his two brothers. All three spent most of the inheritance remodeling their homes in a big way and celebrated with parties. But by the time they got a second inheritance, from their mother, they had different priorities. No more home improvements. The writer put his share straight into college funds for his children.

Of course, most people can't count on a second inheritance. If they're lucky enough to receive even one, they need to make the most of it. At some point, it's time to get real. Except for the ultrarich, most heirs can't do everything they want with their inheritances. They must pick and choose. If you don't want to be an "heirhead," avoid the following inheritance traps.

Spending Large

Receiving an inheritance that substantially improves your finances can be a bit heady. You start believing you can afford a great many things. The thinking goes like this: "I just inherited $300,000, so I can afford to take a little trip . . . and to redecorate the living room . . . and to buy a new car" and so on. You can also succumb to the "if this, then that" syndrome. If I have this much money, then I should be able to afford that. Live like that on a daily basis and you'll soon tap out. Put on the heir brakes!

Here's how I let it happen to me. Early in our marriage my husband and I had no trouble keeping up our mortgage payments, buying new cars when needed, saving in our IRAs, and setting aside a big hunk of savings for my maternity leave before each child was born. We always paid our credit cards off on time.

Since then our income has more than doubled, we've received two inheritances, and yet we struggle at times to pay down balances on credit cards. On the face of it, this makes no sense. But here's how it plays out: If we have so much money, surely it wouldn't hurt for the whole family to accompany our older son when he performs with his choir in New York City. Or on a smaller scale, what's the harm of eating out two or three times a week or buying both kids a book when we go to the bookstore? If we have this much money, then we should be able to live that kind of lifestyle. True, we could dip into our inheritance monies and pay off these debts. But where would it end? Here's the upshot. It's strange but true: As your lifestyle becomes more complex, so do your expenses. If you receive an inheritance, you might need to be more mindful of your spending than ever before.

Underestimating the True Cost

This is also known as, it's not the purchase price, it's the maintenance. Let's say that until you received your inheritance, you were happy driving your three-year-old Camry to work every day. But now that you've inherited $250,000, you decide to indulge your fantasy to drive a Mercedes convertible. True, the price is steep—three times the cost of the Camry—but you plan to plow the rest of the inheritance into retirement savings as you know you should.

The only problem is, you're not considering the true cost of this one luxury. As the car requires maintenance, you will be paying luxury prices for routine checkups, tires, parts, and dent fixing. And, of course, your auto insurance will increase substantially. As the car ages, what then? Was this a one-time joyride or will you feel deprived if you aren't driving a sports car? If you don't generate income for maintenance and replacement elsewhere, you'll have to dip into your retirement savings.

In our case, as we contemplated buying our home, I consulted with our tax advisor on whether we could afford to move from a 1,700-square-foot home to one double that size with a much larger yard. The cost of the house was more than double the old one and the mortgage was three times greater. I factored in the mortgage, the higher property taxes, and the larger home insurance bill. What I wasn't prepared for, frankly, was the maintenance. While the heating bills were actually lower thanks to better construction, the water and gardening bills each month were hefty. And my first trip to Home Depot to buy replacement lightbulbs for the entire house—a $200 proposition—left me gasping for breath at the checkout counter. Would we have decided not to buy, had we known all the costs involved? No, but we might have been better prepared emotionally to do some compensatory trimming of our spending.

Getting Caught on the Consumption Escalator

This is also known as the "Diderot effect," a reference to the eighteenth-century French philosopher Denis Diderot whose essay "Regrets on Parting with My Old

Dressing Gown" aptly describes how today's engine of consumerism works. Diderot's regrets began when he was given a beautiful red dressing gown as a gift. Although he was pleased with this present, he quickly became dissatisfied as he realized how shabby everything else around him seemed by comparison. One by one he replaced everything in his study—desk, curtains, chair, draperies, and shelves. Ultimately, he found himself seated uncomfortably in an elegantly appointed study, wishing he'd never set eyes on that "imperious scarlet robe" that demanded that everything else rise to its standard.

Consumer researchers cite the Diderot effect to describe the ratchetlike movement of modern consumption—always onward and upward, never backward. Buying a new pair of pants, for example, might "necessitate" a new pair of shoes to go with them. The arrival of a new family room couch reveals how old and tattered the nearby rocking chairs are. And a new house, of course, cries out for all new furniture and appointments.

Quitting Your Day Job

When people think about receiving an inheritance, one common fantasy is of leaving their current job. Americans are truly harnessed to a treadmill, working more hours than citizens of any other country. What do we have to show for it? Lots of material goods, a load of consumer debt, and an appalling lack of leisure time.

It's only natural, then, that a bequest inspires daydreams of early retirement or of a less harried and more enjoy-

able kind of work. Your inheritance may be sizable
enough to make this possible, but you should be absolutely certain before you make the switch. Financial
planner Henry E. Zapisek has seen inheritances sap heirs
of their drive and ambition. He urges clients who've inherited money not to give up their careers. "A person's
ability to produce income is still their greatest asset," he
says.

How much would it take to be financially secure? The
cost is probably much higher than you think. Let's say you
inherited $1 million. Back in the 1950s, a cool million
would have bought you a dream house, car, and enough
to live on indefinitely. But to be truly well off today, says
Raajeev Dhawan of the UCLA Anderson Forecasting
Project, takes at least $10 million: $5 million for a house
and cars and servicing them, and $5 million to invest.

What if you don't want the cars and the fancy trap-
pings? How much does it cost to be financially independent? Financial advisor Michael Stolper defines it as
having your house and children's education paid, plus $3
million in investments. The investments would provide
about $180,000 annually in pretax income, enough to live
an upper-middle-class life and enjoy some travel.

Zapisek notes that how much $1 million in liquid as-
sets will do for you depends on your age. "The younger
you are the more money you're going to need," he says.
For example, a couple in their sixties with a home paid off
could probably live on the $3,000 to $4,000 monthly income stream $1 million would safely generate. But a
woman in her fifties who receives a $1 million bequest

and hopes to retire early would probably be disappointed. Running the numbers shows she would run out of money in her seventies and therefore should work another five years. What about a man in his early forties who wants to take his million and retire at forty-five? That escape plan would require $4 million altogether.

Our work often gives us more than money, however. Before you ditch your job, consider how much of your identity is tied up in it. Where else would you find a source of accomplishment and self-esteem? What would you do with your time? I'm not suggesting that you shouldn't use your inheritance to change careers or to retire early. I'm only advising that you proceed with caution so you don't sabotage what could ultimately be a fulfilling and exhilarating change. Remember, you don't have to go cold turkey. You might be able to cut back on your hours or work part time before trying a new career or leaving the workforce altogether. But you must have a well-thought-out plan that takes into account your financial and psychological needs.

Misreading Your Net Worth

Once you've received your inheritance, it's important to calculate your net worth. It isn't that hard or time consuming and will serve as a barometer of how well you're managing your inheritance as time goes on.

On one side of a piece of paper, add up the current value of all your assets: house and any other real estate, investments, savings, retirement plan savings such as 401(k)s and IRAs, cars, and valuables such as artwork and antiques. On the other side, total all your debts: mortgages and home equity lines of credit, auto loans, any personal loans, and all credit card debt. When you subtract the debts from the assets, the balance is your net worth. Ideally, you want to see your net worth grow every year, as your investments appreciate, you pay off debts, and regularly set aside some of your income in savings.

If the addition of your inheritance assets to your own suddenly makes your net worth seem large—as it did for my family—you need to keep this in mind: Some of your assets, though they continue to grow in value, are not liquid assets, like CDs or stocks and bonds. Assets such as a house, summer cabin, or boat, are considered "use" assets. While they can appreciate in value, they cost money to maintain. I received a mixed bag in my inheritance—two houses, two cars, and a painting in addition to cash and stocks. It's not as if someone handed me a check for $500,000. Some of my most valuable assets—our home and our summer cottage—cost us money to keep. If your use assets account for $500,000 of your $800,000 net worth, for example, you have just $300,000 in liquid assets. Bottom line: You could have less readily available money and fewer options than your net worth would indicate.

Failing to Keep Inheritance Funds "Off Limits"

It you're truly committed to preserving and enhancing your inheritance, you must devise a means to keep from frittering it away. For some people, it might be enough to keep assets like money-market funds or stocks in accounts separate from day-to-day check-writing transactions. But these accounts are all too easily accessed with check-writing privileges and borrowing on margin. One inheritor I know kept his inheritance of stocks in a brokerage account, but continually borrowed on margin against them. When this happens, it's time to sit down and decide what you really want to do with the money rather than go on fooling yourself.

It's all too easy to get sucked into spending what should be an "heir-tight" account. After my mother died, I began receiving a $500-a-month annuity as the survivor of her teacher's retirement plan. The rational thing to do with such a gift would be to funnel it directly into a retirement or college saving account without ever touching it. Well, that was certainly my plan.

But in the time following my mother's death, there seemed to be a surplus of turmoil in our lives. Both my in-laws took a turn for the worse, but refused any sort of paid help. Finally we ordered Meals on Wheels for them and footed the bill, using the $500 monthly annuity. When they got better, we used the money for travel and baby-sitting so we could clear out my mother's house and so on. Long story short—that monthly windfall is no longer treated as anything special. It's been absorbed into our regular income, year in and year out.

Behavioral economists tell us that we treat different kinds of money differently, that we compartmentalize. For example, I've dipped into a money-market account containing inherited funds (intending, but not always suc-

ceeding, to repay), but I'm loath to sell off any stock I received. There's a mental moat, if you will, around the
stocks. If you're determined to preserve your inheritance
and to make it grow, then compartmentalization is critical. If necessary, make it difficult to transfer from or write
checks against certain accounts. Then invoke a zero-
withdrawal tolerance.

Failing to Protect Your Assets

If you inherit a car, a boat, or a house, you're going to need
more casualty insurance than you had before. Even if you
plan to sell the property you received, you'll need to protect this asset in the meantime so it retains its worth.

It is also critical at this time to consider purchasing
umbrella insurance, to protect your assets if you are sued.
Although the chances of being sued are small, civil litiga-
tion can strike anyone without warning. And the more
assets you have, the more likely you are to become a target.

"This is the number-one area I see where people are
not covered," says J. Stephen Cowen, a financial planner.
"They've got great life insurance, great health insurance,
but only $100,000 liability on their homes. That's noth-
ing, with today's lawsuits. If you have several hundred
thousand dollars' worth of assets, you desperately need
umbrella insurance."

What kinds of incidents might be covered by an umbrella that wouldn't be under typical homeowner and
auto policies? Here are a few: While away at camp, your

teenage son hosts a party where liquor is served. One of the partygoers later smashes his car into a telephone pole. His family sues you. Or you serve as a director on your neighborhood homeowners association, which has taken the developer to court over building defects. When the suit fails, the homeowners sue you and other directors to recover the legal fees. Or while vacationing in the Swiss Alps, the parking brake on your rental car fails and the car rolls into the ski lodge. The lodge expects you to cover the damages but your auto insurance won't pay. You could be forced to pay a court judgment in any of these cases, even if it means selling most of your assets.

Typically sold in increments of $1 million and $5 million, umbrella policies provide coverage on top of your auto and homeowners insurance, as well as for liabilities not included with other insurance. Coverage can cost as little as $200 annually. Some people are clearly more at risk than others. Most lawsuits against individuals stem from accidents involving either an auto or a home. The more cars and homes you have, the more you need good insurance coverage. Anyone who owns a vacation home, a rental property, or even rents out a room in the home should consider umbrella insurance.

Ignoring the Need to Plan

Achieving the good life doesn't usually happen by itself, say Dwight R. Lee and Richard B. McKenzie, authors of *Getting Rich in America*. Most people find it hard to save or invest in a vacuum. They need goals. Your inheritance won't get you anywhere without some kind of roadmap. By setting goals, you can clarify your thinking and preserve your assets for their highest use. And even if your inheritance has eased certain financial strains, you still need to plan so you can enjoy the better things in life, such as sending your children to college or retiring early to travel.

Lee and McKenzie recommend asking yourself questions like these:

- What is my current job? What do I want it to be in one year, five years, and ten years?
- What is my annual income? What do I want it to be a year from now, five years from now, ten years?
- What is my net worth? What should it be when I retire?
- How much do I save each year? What is my savings goal for next year? Then write briefly how you intend to achieve your goals—career, income, net worth, savings—over these time periods. Revisit these goals at least once a year.

Giving In to Procrastination

Even with the boost an inheritance can provide it's hard to get started on financial planning for large goals like retirement and college. Despite our best intentions, these major goals are often crowded out by immediate daily concerns. You might even have thought that if you only had another $50,000 or $100,000 you wouldn't dread financial planning. Well, now you've inherited some money and you still hate the thought.

Procrastination is one of the most common reasons people fail to achieve their financial goals, says financial advisor Mark Dowling. "But the things you're trying to beat, like inflation, don't procrastinate."

Here are the most common excuses and how to vanquish them:

- I'll do it later. I've got plenty of time.

  In fact, time is your ally but only if you put it to work. The earlier you start, the less money you'll need to set aside. Here's how it works. Consider the "do-it-now" investor who faithfully contributes $2,000 a year into an IRA account for ten years for a total of $20,000. She invests no more but lets the account grow annually at a rate of 8 percent for another twenty-five years until it has grown to $214,295. Now for the "put-it-off" investor who waits ten years before starting to invest. He then contributes $2,000 annually to an IRA, also earning 8 percent annually, for the next twenty-five years. While he has contributed a hefty $50,000, his account has just $157,909. Behold the almost magical power of compounding.

- This is a bad time to invest. The market is so low—I'm afraid it will fall even farther. The market is too high—I worry it will crash. The market is too volatile.

  Innumerable uncertainties can hurt the stock market, such as a scandal in the White House, an energy crisis, a war in the Middle East, or a presidential election year. But it's the long course of the market's progress, not the day-to-day swings, that you want to monitor. Over the long term—at least ten or twenty years—the stock market rises. And it outperforms every other kind of investment security. Time in the market is the key, not timing the market.

One way to overcome market anxiety is to practice dollar-cost averaging. Typically an investor buys stocks or mutual funds periodically, say each month, using a set amount of money. The regular monthly purchases allow the investor to buy more shares when the price is low and fewer shares when the price is high—a win-win situation. If the market is up, so is the investment. If the market is down, the investor is buying cheap stock that will rebound when the market does—as it always has. Workers who invest in 401(k) and 403(b) retirement plans are practicing dollar-cost averaging—and compounding their earnings tax-deferred.

- I've got too little to invest.

But even a small amount invested early and with regularity can add up. Invest just $100 a month in a mutual fund earning 10 percent (the long-term annualized return on stocks), and after five years, the investment has grown to $7,907. But after ten years, it has grown to $20,754. And after thirty-five years, that modest $100 a month set aside has swelled with compounding to $382,926. "The important thing is to get started and get in the habit of doing it," says Dowling. "Make it as simple as you can so it becomes automatic."

• I'm just too busy right now.

Financial planners can't help but be frustrated by the fact that many people spend more time planning their summer vacation than planning their finances. Is it more important to plan for your kid's college education or to go to a movie? Consider the relative importance of what you do day to day. Ask yourself how much time it takes you to earn $10,000. How much time do you spend figuring out a way for that $10,000 to work for you?

• Financial planning scares me. I feel overwhelmed just thinking about it.

Financial phobia is all too common. Most adults are embarrassed to admit any shortcomings, believing they should somehow have learned all about money and investing when they were young (even though the subject wasn't taught in school). Often, too, those who are successful in their careers feel badly that they don't know how to create a stock portfolio. However, making money and managing it are two different skills.

And of course we are bombarded with frightening statistics warning of the high cost of retirement and college. The situation can seem so dire that some people simply give up. But if you strive to get organized a little at a time, your confidence will increase. You might ultimately find that you can't achieve all your goals and must temper your expectations. But, surprisingly, financial advisors report that there is a certain satisfaction in defining what you can and can't do.

Not Doing Your Own Estate Planning

Do you want your second wife's children to get your inheritance instead of your own kids? Or do you want your money to go to a favorite charity and not to your worthless brother? Maybe you'd like to make inheriting easier for your heirs than it was for you. If so, you need to devise an estate plan. (See Chapter 13, Planning Your Own Estate.) If the thought of doing this has been nagging at you, you may be surprised at how relieved you feel to get it done.

Failing to Seek Professional Help

It always amazes me that people who would never dream of rewiring the electrical outlets in their house or replacing the carburetor on their car will fail to seek financial help. As a society, we believe we should know how to manage money because it's such a part of our everyday lives. Well, so are light sockets and cars, but I'll rely on electricians and mechanics to help me with major repairs. Hiring professionals (see Chapter 11, Getting Professional Help) to assist you with your investing, taxes, and estate planning should greatly help maximize your inheritance.

Chapter 10

Go Fish Finance 101

How do you make a million? You start with $900,000.
—Stephen Lewis

Your inheritance is something that was given to you. To make the most of it, you need to move from the passive role of recipient to the active role of manager. The assets you've inherited might feel like hand-me-down clothing—they were meant to fit someone else. At the end of their lives, for example, your parents might have sought safety and security by putting their money in certificates of deposit and bonds. Also they were probably holding tight to a sizable nest egg, the equity in the home they owned free and clear. But unlike your parents, who enjoyed reliable corporate pension plans, you need growth investments as well as income-producing investments in your self-directed retirement plans. And if you live in New York, you'll have little use for that family homestead in the Chicago suburbs. That's why you must tailor the assets you receive so that they suit you.

To maximize your inheritance, you need a financial plan. Don't think of this as a collection of dry-as-dust numbers, but a road map, if you will, to your goals. Your goals are both the end and the means. They are what motivate you to stick with your savings plan. It's hard to save and invest in a vacuum. Your inheritance may allow you to send your children or grandchildren to a top-notch college or permit you to retire early and travel. But you need to make certain your money is working optimally.

Jeanne Bradford-Odorico, a financial planner, says she strives to have her clients establish clearly defined and realistic goals. "When people feel that they're going somewhere, they start to see some results. They feel empowered."

You don't have to be your own money manager. If investing makes you nervous or unhappy, delegate it to someone else. In fact, I strongly recommend working with a financial advisor. But never give up oversight. And for that you must understand the basics of financial planning.

When I've interviewed financial advisors over the years, I've always looked for those who possess not just knowledge, but wisdom, the kind of person who'll not only help you invest successfully for early retirement, but will take the time to ask you if that's really what you want to do and how you'll keep busy. In this chapter, I'll draw on all that accumulated wisdom to give you my Go Fish Heiress Finance 101.

One caveat, however, before we start. The assets you've inherited could carry some emotional baggage that hampers your ability to maximize them (See Chapter

7, From the Grave), so start by acknowledging and dealing with them.

THE PROBLEM WITH HAND-ME-DOWN MONEY

YOUR PARENTS' INVESTMENTS might not be a good fit for you. For example, they probably had a different risk-tolerance zone. In their later years, your parents might have done little if any stock investing, preferring the safety and security of fixed-income investments such as CDs and Treasury bonds. You, however, probably have a higher tolerance for risk. If you're near the middle of your life rather than the end, you need growth in your investments. Stocks and real estate, as well as some income investments, fit the bill.

Also your parents were probably in a different tax bracket from you. In retirement, they might have been in a low tax bracket, so holding taxable income-producing investments was not a problem. But when you inherit these, the income from them could propel you into a higher bracket, cut you off from certain tax breaks such as the Roth IRA, and put you at risk of paying the onerous alternative minimum tax. You'll need to consider some tax-advantaged approaches, such as holding income-producing investments inside tax-sheltered 401(k)s and IRAs, and investing in stocks with high appreciation and little income in your taxable accounts.

Start with Protection

Before deciding how to best to use your inheritance to reach your goals, you need to protect what you have. To use a sports analogy, investing is your offense, the way to score points, or add to your assets. But every offense needs a good defense, to ensure that what is accumulated won't be lost out of carelessness. Your defense is a risk management plan, consisting of several key types of insurance:

- **Health insurance.** It's essential that you and your family have adequate health insurance that covers hospitalization and major illness. Without insurance, your week in the hospital could easily wipe out your emergency savings. And a catastrophic illness could erase your family's financial security. Usually the best source of insurance is through an employer benefits plan. Those without employer plans should consult an experienced independent insurance agent who can shop from among a variety of insurers.

- **Life insurance.** Not everyone needs life insurance— it's necessary only if you have others dependent on you for support or you want to use it for estate planning purposes. If you are the parent of an underage child or if anyone else relies on you for financial support, then you could probably require a good amount of it. What you hope to accomplish with insurance is to replace the income that would be lost for only the numbers of years it would be needed. Calculating how much you need can be tricky. But the most straightforward method I've seen is offered by Eric Tyson, author of many bestselling Dummies personal finance books. First, keep in mind that you are replacing after-tax money because life insurance proceeds are not taxed.

So you can either figure your after-tax income using your most recent tax return or derive it this way: Multiply your gross income by 80 percent if you're a low income earner, 70 percent for a moderate-income earner or 60 percent for a high income earner. Then estimate the number of years that the income would be needed. If the number of years is five, multiply your after-tax income by 4.5, if it is 10 years, by 8.5; if 20 years, by 15 and if 30 years, by 20. Thus, someone with a $60,000 after-tax income and a need for 10 years of insurance would require $510,000 worth of life insurance.

Coverage is essential not just for a working parent, but for stay-at-home parents. While they might bring in little or no income, it would be costly to hire others to fill in for their child-care, housecleaning and cooking duties.

For most people hoping to provide insurance for a spouse and children, low-cost term insurance is the way to go. You can use the services of an independent insurance agent, who will shop different carriers for you, or try comparison shopping on the Internet, which is not necessarily cheaper. To obtain insurance quotes, visit these websites: QuickQuote at *www.quickquote.com*, Quotesmith.com at *www.quotesmith.com* and Selectquote at *www.selectquote.com*. No matter where you buy your insurance, be certain to purchase from an insurer with the highest "A" ratings from major rating services, such as A. M. Best (*www.ambest.com*), Weiss Ratings (*www.weissratings.com*) and Moody's Investors Services (*www.moodys.com*).

- **Disability.** Most of us think nothing of insuring our home or car. But what about the income that pays for them? You are more likely to become disabled than to die. That's why every breadwinner should try, if possible, to have disability insurance. Such coverage replaces a portion of your income—say 60 percent— while you recover from your disability. The least expensive plans are available through benefits plans at large corporations. The self-employed can sometimes buy them through trade or professional associations. Otherwise, individual policies can be expensive, though necessary. Use an experienced, independent insurance broker who can shop different companies for the best policies.

- **Property and liability insurance.** It's prudent to carry as much insurance on your car as you can. One accident with injuries can run into hundreds of thousands of dollars. In covering your home, you want to be certain your insurance will pay for the complete replacement cost. After all, your home is one of your biggest assets. Every few years, have your agent determine if your coverage is still adequate. In addition you probably need umbrella insurance, or general liability insurance, to protect your assets should you be sued for events not covered by your home and auto insurers or for amounts above those coverages. "If you're driving down the freeway in the fog and you hit a surgeon, your $100,000 to $300,000 maximum liability won't even cover the attorney's fees," says Timothy J. Clyman, a certified financial planner. (For more on umbrella insurance, see Chapter 9, Get Real.)

Finally, one more thing before you move from defense to offense with your inheritance. You could be carrying around some extra weight that will act as a drag on your plans, namely high-interest consumer debt. If you had trouble keeping it under control before your inheritance, the situation could get worse after you receive it. You might feel, understandably, that you've never had more money in your life and that if you go a little wild now there's no harm done.

The problem with credit card debt, however, is you didn't just spend the money. You borrowed to spend it. Credit card debt is insidious. It can gradually undermine your financial security. Not only do you have to repay what you borrowed, you must pay interest at high rates. To repay $1,000 borrowed at 18 percent interest with the minimum payment required would take more than nineteen years and cost $1,931.11 in interest.

PLASTIC REALITIES

ALTHOUGH CARD ISSUERS, responding to years of interest rate cuts by the Federal Reserve, have lowered their rates in recent years to the benefit of customers, they've also introduced a practice roundly criticized by consumer advocates. Card companies have reduced the minimum required payment from around 4 percent of the balance owed to 2 percent, thus stretching out the repayment period. That might sound insignificant, but this can lull borrowers into feeling they don't owe much, based on the smaller monthly payments. The upshot—cardholders could charge even more, take longer to repay, and end up owing more interest.

Credit card companies also make it difficult to pay off debt, though it might appear just the opposite. Most issuers have you pay off debt in order of interest rate—your monthly payment goes to pay off the lowest-rate debt first and the highest-rate debt last, no matter when the transactions occurred. If you take advantage of a short-term low-rate or even zero-rate offer to transfer other card balances, those will be repaid first. Meanwhile your higher rate debt, such as the cash withdrawal you made three years ago at a rate of 18 percent, sits at the back end of your bill racking up interest while you pile up more on the front end. And your lower-interest-rate debt could become higher-rate debt if you are late on your monthly payment and incur a penalty rate.

You might decide to pay off your consumer debt using your inheritance or by refinancing the mortgage on your home and taking cash out. However, it's not enough to pay it off. You must have a change of heart and a change of behavior. Otherwise your debts will creep back up. It's bad enough to have to use your windfall to pay off old debts, but to see the debt recurring is depressing. If you can't figure out where all your money is going, keep a daily log of family expenses on everything you spend for one month. Certain patterns are bound to emerge, such as the $20 a month in video late fees and $75 a month on café lattes. Adding these up can provide enough of a jolt to change these habits. As a long-term goal, aim to use your credit cards for convenience and for bonus programs, not to spend money you don't have.

Not all debt is bad. Borrowing (in moderation, of course) to acquire something that will create value can be a good thing. The most common examples include buying a home, which not only provides a place to live but has the potential to increase in monetary value, and taking out student loans to complete an education, which in theory allows students to earn more throughout life and to enjoy personal growth. Taking out a loan to start a business is another. Bad debt is paying for something you consume. It's the $60 dinner out you had last year. If left on your credit card, it could wind up costing double that by the time you pay it off, long after you can recall what you ordered.

How the Pros Invest

When given a lump sum of money, many people look at the vast number of potential investments and worry how to invest it and how they can make the greatest return. Good financial advisors, however, look at this issue in a somewhat different way. They narrow the universe of acceptable investments by considering the following issues:

- **Time horizon**. This is probably the single most important criterion in selecting an investment. Will you need this money in the short term, say within the next five years? If you're saving up to buy a house in a year, for example, your down-payment savings belong with the stability of a money-market fund or a short-term bond fund, not in the stock market, where it could suffer a 20- to 30-percent hit just as you need it. Or can your money stay invested for the long term, ten years or more? If you're investing for a retirement that's twenty years away, you need your money to grow. That means putting the bulk of it in stocks, knowing you have time to recover from major market downturns.

- **Risk tolerance**. Assessing your risk tolerance can be tricky if you've never actively participated in the stock and bond markets during a downturn. It's hard to know what you would do in a hypothetical situation. Many novice investors who enjoyed double-digit returns on their high-tech portfolios in the late 1990s failed to understand that stocks capable of climbing by 40 percent one year can also plunge by 40 percent the next. Stocks that offer the greatest returns in the long run are volatile—that is, they fluctuate up and down. Investments with low volatility like bonds offer lower returns. Thus we have the risk-reward trade-off. The question is: How will you feel if some of your investments drop by 30 percent and stay there for two or more years? Will you panic, or can you stay the course? It is possible for relatively unsophisticated investors to ride out rough times, especially if they have a trusted financial advisor to educate and counsel them.

- **Investment costs**. Whether you rely on mutual funds or hire a financial advisor to manage your investments, you need to be aware of your investment costs. For mutual funds, the cost ranges from as little as .15 of 1 percent of your investments annually to more than 2 percent, with 1.4 percent being typical. Depending on how much money is under management and what services are provided, a financial advisor could charge fees as low as 1 percent or less and as much as 3 percent or more. (The greater the size of your portfolio, the lower the fee, in general.)

Over the long haul, higher fees can be a significant drain on your investment. Here's an example offered by the Vanguard Group, the low-cost pioneer in the mutual fund industry: A one-time investment of $25,000 earning 10 percent annually compounded over twenty years in a fund with a fee, or expense ratio, of 1.3 percent will earn $31,701 less than the same investment in a fund with an expense ratio of just .2 percent.[1] This is why many financial advisors make low-cost index mutual funds like those offered by Vanguard the foundation of client investment portfolios.

- **Taxes**. When investors take profits on their investments, they owe capital gains taxes (as opposed to income taxes). There are two kinds of capital gains, short-term and long term. With short-term gains, or those held less than one year, investors must pay at their personal income tax rate. If you paid $10,000 for stock and you decide to sell it eleven months later when the value has risen to $12,000, your capital gain is $2,000. Assuming you're in the 30 percent federal tax bracket, you would owe $600 at tax time. But had you waited one year and one day (assuming the stock held its $12,000 value), you'd pay at the lower long-term rate of 20 percent (or even lower for those in the lowest brackets), or $400.

Many mutual funds generate high short-term gains because fund managers buy and sell in an effort to boost returns. A KPMG Peat Marwick study found that between 1987 and 1997 taxes cost the typical mutual fund shareholder 16 percent in annual total returns.[2] To help investors better gauge this drain on returns, in 2001 the Securities and Exchange Commission began requiring funds to include after-tax returns in their annual reports and prospectuses.

• **Liquidity and flexibility**. Many investments are highly liquid; that is, you could sell them quickly for cash if you needed. These include the stocks and bonds traded on major exchanges and mutual funds. But some of the best places to hold these investments will penalize you for taking out too much money or taking it out too early. This is the trade-off for getting the tax benefits from 401(k) retirement plans, IRA accounts, and annuities. So before you commit funds, be certain you won't need the money in the near term and that you know the rules, which can and do change often.

For example, most companies allow employees to borrow from their retirement plans. But it's a hazardous practice—most plans require employees who are laid off to repay the loans quickly or else pay taxes and penalties that can run as high as 50 percent of the borrowed amount.

LUMP IT AND LIKE IT

MANY INHERITORS ARE given a lump sum of money that they'd like to invest in the stock market. But they face a dilemma. Should they invest it all at once and run the risk the market will tank, or should they plow it in over time? If you find yourself in this situation, try not to fret about whether the market is too high or too low. Almost no one can time the market in this way. Just remember that over the long haul the market goes up and not down. So the odds are that plunking your money down all at once is the better choice. However, financial advisors know that few investors have the stomach for this approach, and so recommend entering the market by stages over months or years. This is a practice known as dollar-cost averaging. You can ask your financial advisor or mutual fund to make the investments automatically. Should you begin investing this way and the market goes down, don't feel badly. You're buying stocks on sale.

Equity versus Income

When you invest your money, you can be either a buyer or a lender. As a buyer in the stock of a company, you are an equity holder, hoping to benefit from your investment's appreciation. The appreciation can be substantial over time, with no upside limit. However, the value can go down as well as up.

As a lender, however, you are seeking income from bonds, certificates of deposit, or money-market funds.

Generally, you get back what you put in, plus interest. These investments have limited upside return, but offer more certainty and less volatility.

Over the past two centuries, stocks held for the long term have handily outperformed bonds, according to Jeremy J. Siegel, professor of finance at the Wharton School of the University of Pennsylvania and author of *Stocks for the Long Run*. From 1802 to 1997, through two World Wars, the industrial revolution, and the computer age, Siegel found that stocks returned an average of 10.2 percent, for a 7 percent real return; that is, the return after inflation. With a 7 percent return investors can double their money every ten years. By comparison, the real (after inflation) rate of return on long-term bonds from 1926 to 1997 was 2 percent. At 2 percent, it takes investors forty years to double their money. Siegel concludes: "The dominance of stocks over fixed-income securities is overwhelming for investors with long horizons."[3]

Unless stocks make up at least 30 to 40 percent of a long-term portfolio, it will probably not keep pace with inflation, says John Markese, president of the American Association of Individual Investors in Chicago. The biggest threat for most people investing for retirement or college is not the day-to-day fluctuation in the market, he says: "The real risk is failure to meet the goal."

What this means to the average investor is this: If you are investing for a goal at least ten years away (and better still, fifteen years away), and if you can watch the markets plunge without panicking, you should invest most of your money in the stock market. Not that you don't need some fixed-income investments as well. But you should think of those as ship's ballast and your stocks as its sails, says financial planner Ginita Wall. The farther out you need to sail toward your goals, the less ballast you'll need.

So what's the best mix of stocks to income investments? That all depends on your time horizon and your risk tolerance. But a good starting point is the 60–40 benchmark. For decades this has been the standard used by managers of traditional pension funds, who relied on the 60 percent in stocks for growth and the 40 in bonds to ensure stability. If you're investing for your own retirement and have many years ahead of you, you can afford to adjust the ratio to 70–30, 80–20, even 90–10—if you're confident you can stay the course. But if your goal is nearer, say ten years before a child enters college, or you're more risk averse, then you could alter the ratio to favor fixed income. But it's likely you will have to save more to reach your goal.

Asset Allocation

Investors have long assumed that diversification helped reduce risk. In recent decades, Nobel Prize–winning economists have measured and described how diversification can be used to maximize return and minimize risk. They concluded that it was possible to design portfolios to achieve a certain result based on the historical performances of asset classes—such as large-company stocks, international stocks, or bonds. How well a portfolio does, they said, depends not on the individual stocks or bonds chosen, but almost entirely on the asset classes. This investment outlook downplays the art of stock picking and emphasizes the utility of index funds.

When considering your investments, try not to compartmentalize them, but make them work together. For example, if you have investments within your 401(k) plan at work and also in a taxable account that you manage, you need to coordinate their duties. Try to include your fixed-income investments in your 401(k) or IRA if possible, so the income they generate will grow tax-deferred. You taxable account is a more suitable place for a mutual fund comprised of small company stocks that offer no dividends but rather the possibility of appreciation—which would not be taxed until you sell the stocks, and even then under the more favorable long-term capital gains rate. Also, make certain your portfolio is truly diversified. Many novice investors have bought several different mutual funds only to realize later they hadn't diversified at all. Each fund held the same kind of stocks.

THE PLAIN-VANILLA PLAN, PLEASE

THE LONGER I write about money, the more convinced I become that investing is less complicated than most people make it out to be. Some people, often those with a financial product to sell, will insist that only professionals can fathom the complexities. But in my role as a personal finance columnist, I've encountered some renowned experts who make investing sound disarmingly simple.

One is Jane Bryant Quinn, the first lady of personal finance, whom I interviewed twice in recent years. In an age of specialized investing in such products as exchange-traded funds and hedge funds, she seemed to delight in sharing the straightforward manner in which she has set up her investment portfolio. A few years ago, she had her no-frills portfolio in five types of mutual funds: S&P 500 index, Treasuries or municipal bonds, small companies or small cap, international stocks, and emerging markets. "My view is, put it in regularly and leave it there," she says. "Wake up in twenty years. It's real easy. The point is consistency, regularity, and keeping your costs down." Ignore the human impulse to buy and sell. While it's true that we're burdened with financial information overload, she says, "there is a simple investment plan in there trying to get out."

Another expert is Harry Markowitz, winner of the 1990 Nobel Prize in economics for his work in investment theory, who lives not far from me. After this brilliant yet modest man spent an hour detailing his mathematical theory on a white board in his office, I finally had my chance to ask: How did this illustrious thinker, employed by large international investment companies to get the edge on the markets, manage his own investment portfolio? "We don't do much [that is] analytic around the house," he confessed. "It's just too much fuss." His retirement portfolio has long been invested in plain vanilla mutual funds, half in stocks and half in bonds. Call it the brain's no-brainer approach. He suggested that investors rely on diversified no-load funds, that is, index funds, then let compounding work its magic.

Major Life Goals

Financing an important goal that is years away, such as college for your kids or your own retirement, feels a lot like shooting at a moving target. How can you know when your child is ten if she will even want to go to college when the time comes? Or whether she might get in on a basketball scholarship? As for retirement, the unknowns are many. Will you be in good health? Will you be forced to retire early? Will Social Security be there to supplement your savings?

Such uncertainties make long-term planning a challenge. But you must nevertheless take aim at your target. I've listed some common life goals below and suggested approaches.

- **Buying a home.** Your inheritance might allow you to buy a home—perhaps bigger, newer, or in a more desirable location than your current residence. This can be a rewarding way to enjoy your inheritance, but be mindful of overspending, both on the purchase price and on the cost of upkeep. Will the house make it difficult for you to help your children go to college or for you to retire?

SHOULD I PAY OFF THE MORTGAGE BEFORE I RETIRE?

THAT WAS GENERALLY how our parents' generation did it. Many people today still want the security of owning a home free and clear, and will strive to pay off their mortgages prior to retirement. But a growing number of middle-aged Americans are taking on mortgages that will have them making payments when they're in their seventies and eighties. A 2002 survey by Allstate Financial found that 27 percent of baby boomers expect to owe on a home mortgage during retirement.⁴

This isn't necessarily a bad thing, say financial advisors. Before you start paying off your mortgage early, run the numbers. "If we just look at the simple math," says financial advisor Sheryl Rowling, "you're better off with a thirty-year mortgage and investing the savings." If you're in the 35 percent federal and state tax bracket and have a 7 percent mortgage, repaying your mortgage early provides a return of 4.5 percent. Assuming you're invested in stocks for the long term, says Rowling, history shows you'd earn 6.5 percent after taxes—a difference of 2 percentage points. Les Merrithew, a financial planner and a baby boomer who took out a thirty-year mortgage in his early fifties, says, "I don't think there's ever a need to pay off your mortgage. Our generation is much more tolerant of risk and, to some degree, more analytical. Most will pick greater returns over security."

- **Buying a vacation home (or maintaining one you inherited).** Like many families, yours might have dreamed of owning a family vacation home at the shore or up in the mountains. With an inheritance, that dream could become a reality, either because you inherit one or you receive enough money to make buying one possible. If you plan to purchase a second home, conduct a reality check first. If your plan depends on your renting the home out part of the year, are you prepared for the hassle and responsibilities of being a landlord? Do you have sufficient funds to cover expenses if you can't find renters? Keep in mind that if you want the most lucrative tax breaks for holding the property as a rental, says CPA Curt J. Welker, you and your family can stay there generally no more than 14 days a year.

If you inherit a summer (or winter) home, how practical is it for you to keep? Is it a long distance and many hours from your primary home? Even if the property has little or no mortgage debt, it can still be a major financial drain. A home, whether or not you use it all year, still needs maintenance. The roof wears out, the wood decks rot, and the pipes leak even when you're not there.

Owning a second home (assuming, unlike mine, it's livable year-round) can help you employ a lucrative tax-saving strategy, however. Some people buy a vacation property in a place where they would like to retire, with the idea of getting acclimated. Thanks to a recent tax change that greatly liberalized the rules governing capital gains on the sale of primary residences, homeowners can now qualify for a sizable tax exemption more than once. When you sell your principal residence (a place you have lived for the past two of the previous five years), you are exempt from paying capital gains on your profit up to $250,000 if you are single and up to $500,000 if you are married. When you move to your retirement home, you can sell if you like after two years and use the exemption again, although taxes will be owed if you took certain tax breaks for renting it out. Of it you decide in the long run to sell your vacation home, you can live there two years, sell it, take the tax break, and return to your regular home. The possibilities are many for people no longer tied down by their work.

- **College**. For middle- and upper-middle-class families, saving for college can seem a daunting task. Unlike the wealthy, who can foot the bill for the rising cost of a college degree, or those with modest incomes, who can qualify for financial aid, the middle class must rely mainly on saving and borrowing. Fortunately, the 2001 Economic Growth and Tax Relief Reconciliation Act greatly enhanced the ability of families to save and invest. The two principal methods are 529 plans, also known as college state savings, and education savings accounts.

  The 529 plans are the heavy hitters. They allow families to contribute large sums (as much as $250,000 in some states) to investment accounts overseen by individual states and managed by investment companies like Vanguard and TIAA-CREF. Anyone, whether parent, grandfather, or friend, can open an account on behalf of a beneficiary using any plan offered in the country. Control remains with the person who opened the account, and it can be used for alternate beneficiaries. The funds grow tax-free. As long as the money is used for qualified educational expenses, no federal

tax (and no state taxes in many states) will be due when
it is withdrawn. (That could change after 2010, unless
Congress acts to preserve this feature.) How much can
you save with these plans? As much as 33 percent more
over eighteen years than with a taxable account.

Education savings accounts, once known as Education IRAs, have gotten a welcome makeover. Annual contributions per beneficiary under age eighteen
have been raised from $500 to $2,000, enough to make
them worthwhile. And income limits for contributors
have been raised to $95,000 a year adjusted gross in-
come for single persons and $190,000 for married cou-
ples. As with the 529 plans, the money withdrawn is
tax free if used for education. Unlike the plans, though,
investments are entirely self-directed.

Even with these tools, few families will simply be
able to write a check for four years in college when the
time comes. It can be helpful to look at your contribution to your child's college education as you would
a down payment on a house. Certainly four years at
some private colleges cost enough to buy a house.
View it as something of great value that will take time
and effort to pay off. You will probably have to rely on
a variety of sources, such as savings, loans, and your
child's contribution from working.

• **Retirement.** Receiving an inheritance can certainly
   help kick-start your retirement savings. It might even
   encourage you to think about early retirement.
   Fortunately, the 2001 tax relief act has given retirement
   savers a big boost. The maximum contribution em-

ployees can make to their 401(k) and 403(b) plans rises by $1,000 annually from $11,000 in 2002 to $15,000 in 2006 and thereafter. Workers age fifty and older can also make "catch-up" contributions starting at $1,000 in 2002 and increasing by $1,000 each year until they reach $5,000 in 2006 and thereafter. The limits on IRAs have been raised as well—to $3,000 for the years 2002–2004, $4,000 for the years 2006 and 2007, and $5,000 for years 2008 and after. Catch-up provisions apply here as well: $500 a year between 2002 and 2005 and $1,000 a year starting in 2006.

Try to funnel as much of your retirement savings as you can into tax-advantaged accounts like those above. The tax break helps your money work harder.

When planning for retirement keep in mind:

- Whether you retire early or late, you should plan for longevity. Many of us will be living into our eighties and nineties, nearly a second lifetime after retirement. We should prepare, Gail Sheehy, author of the *Passages* books once told me in an interview, to be so old that we'll forget the name of our first spouse and see our grandsons go bald.
- Not many people will be able to afford early retirement because of the considerable cost. If you quit the workforce at age fifty-five, you are losing a decade of earnings and savings, as well as gaining ten years of spending. Working part time into traditional retirement years will be a popular option for many boomers.

- Maximize your 401(k) plan. Take full advantage of company matching funds.
- Don't let your employer's stock make up more than 10 percent of retirement savings. If the company fell on hard times, you could be doubly hit—laid off from your job and stuck with a decimated retirement fund.

RECOMMENDED READING

FOR MORE INFORMATION on investing and personal finance, I recommend the following books:

Investing Bible by Lynn O'Shaughnessy (John Wiley & Sons), *www.wiley.com*

Retirement Bible by Lynn O'Shaughnessy (John Wiley & Sons), *www.wiley.com*

Personal Finance for Dummies by Eric Tyson (John Wiley & Sons), *www.wiley.com*

Investing for Dummies by Eric Tyson (John Wiley & Sons), *www.wiley.com*

Financing College by Kristin Davis (Kiplinger Books), *www.kiplinger.com*

Retire Worry Free by the Staff of *Kiplinger's Personal Finance* magazine (Kiplinger Books), *www.kiplinger.com*

Which Comes First?

Saving for your retirement or saving for your children's college education? Baby boomer parents often fret over which to favor. Many of us tend to focus on college because it usually arrives before our retirement and because we're conditioned to put our children's interest before our own.

But many financial advisors say it should be the other way around, with the emphasis on our retirement. I call it the "oxygen-mask" approach: Place the mask on yourself, then help your child. Here's why. Although we parents can borrow at relatively low rates for college using student loans or home equity lines, nobody's going to lend us money to finance our retirement. (Unless you count the reverse mortgage on the family home, not yet a wildly popular retirement product.) Retirement income simply must come from pensions and from savings. Cutting the costs of college, however, can be accomplished in various ways, such as having a child finish a four-year college in three years, or stretch out course work to five years thereby allowing more time to work, or attend a less expensive community college for two years then switch to a more prestigious university for the final two years and the name diploma.

Most retirement saving is done through tax-advantaged 401(k) plans and IRAs, which can provide immediate tax breaks as well as enhanced investment returns thanks to their tax-deferred status. Some tax benefits you receive for funding a college education are based on the after-tax dollars spent on college tuition and fees, whether from income or borrowing. In addition, when considering whether to award financial aid, many colleges do not count parental retirement accounts as assets that could be tapped.

And finally, it's reasonable for you to expect your children to work to help pay for college, which is likely to help them value a college education even more. Besides, you can't always say "yes" to your child. Joan Cudhea, a financial planner, says that parents should not feel guilty about stockpiling their retirement funds: "I think it's a gift to your child to assure them you won't run out of money in retirement."

Chapter 11

Getting Professional Help

Believe one who has proved it. Believe an expert.
—Virgil

Whin I first spoke to Wendy, the inheritor from Chapter 7 whose net worth is tied up in one stock left by her father, she was grappling with how to handle her finances. "Right now it occupies a very large part of my brain," she said. In an effort to cope, she had recently subscribed to several financial magazines. "I'm overwhelmed with information. I'm just getting a grip on terms like 'mid-cap.'" What Wendy really wanted, she told me, was to throw away all the magazines, find a financial advisor, and develop a five-year plan.

Getting Professional Help

Once you receive an inheritance, you are likely to need some kind of professional help whether it's managing your finances, valuing and protecting your assets, or putting your own legal affairs in order. Unfortunately, you could be an easy mark for all kinds of advisors hoping to get their share of the great wealth-transfer pie. And if you are grieving or overwhelmed, you could be vulnerable and not at your most vigilant.

Although it might not be obvious at first, you could well need an entire team of advisors, depending on the nature and complexity of your inheritance. In my own situation, I eventually sought the help of a certified financial planner, an estate planning attorney, and several patent attorneys (regarding Go Fish). Prior to the inheritance, we had used a tax preparer and occasionally I did our tax returns myself. But the inheritance dramatically complicated our financial lives and I needed the help of a top-notch accountant. I also had to hire an appraiser to value several paintings, and a real estate appraiser for the cabin in Michigan.

The most common and the most damaging mistake I see people make is failing to spend money up front for professional advice that would save them much more later on. Every year my newspaper conducts personal finance hotlines staffed by financial experts, usually certified financial planners or certified public accountants, to answer questions from readers. It never fails at each hotline that one or more multimillionaires call in for some free advice. (Not that the experts are stingy with their advice, they just can't understand why such affluent people would be so shortsighted.) After walking a wealthy doctor through his complicated tax form by phone, one accountant hung up the phone, threw her hands up in the air, and said,

"Do I do my own anesthesiology? No!" Tax planning, rather than getting a complex tax return done by phone for free, would be more likely to save the doctor money in the long run.

Many people balk at paying financial fees or commissions, because in their minds these "cost too much." Yet a good financial planner could save them many thousands of dollars in the future by selecting sound investments, choosing investments with low fees and low tax costs, and helping preserve current assets. An astute CPA, who can charge $200 an hour or more, should be able to save you in taxes at least as much as his or her fee. A knowledgeable estate planning attorney should not only protect your heirs from estate taxes, but also provide you with peace of mind.

While you shouldn't be afraid to spend money for good advice, neither should you walk in flashing a sign that essentially says "new heir—easy money." Unfortunately, there are advisors out there who will hear the word "inheritance" and size you up as a mark, someone with a lump sum who hasn't got a clue what to do with it. Financial institutions across the country have been positioning themselves for years to enjoy a bite of your windfall. Some can get aggressive about it.

Don't be ashamed to demonstrate from the beginning that you are cost conscious. Trust me, you won't come across as a rube if you show you care about costs. And if an advisor makes you feel that way, then they aren't going to do the job you need them to do—protect and grow your money. Many wealthy people got where they are because they're not afraid to question whether they're getting good value.

How much money do you need to have before seeking advice? The Phoenix Affluent American study of 1996 found that only one in five investors would feel a need for financial advice if they had $10,000 in assets. But nine out of ten said they would need help for investments of $100,000 or more.[1] Clearly, individuals feel more intimidated by larger sums of money. And they probably worry that they have more to lose as the numbers grow. It's unfortunate, however, that those who have $10,000 or $50,000 don't feel the same urgency to seek help. Having less, they need to try to make the most of it. It's true that some financial advisors and investment firms will not accept you as a client if you don't have, say $300,000 or $500,000, in investable assets. But don't get discouraged. Remember that the advisors who run those firms were once starting out and taking clients like you. Just find the next generation.

ONE-STOP FINANCES?

INHERITORS COULD BE among the biggest beneficiaries of a dramatic trend in the financial services industry. Because of an abundant supply of financial advisors, consolidation is under way. The result is likely to be better advice to consumers at a cheaper price, says Mark Hurley, chairman of the Dallas mutual fund company Undiscovered Managers and author of a study on the industry. In just a few years, predicts Hurley, consumers will be able to sign on with a firm that will include specialists to help them select insurance, do their income taxes, offer advice on educating their children about money, and help them determine if they're getting paid enough for their work. And it will cost less than the individual services combined would have five years earlier.

This one-stop-shopping approach could hold some appeal, especially for inheritors, who are likely to need a variety of services. But there are downsides. A client might like the firm's estate planning attorney but feel uncomfortable confiding in the financial planner. Yet trust is key in this kind of relationship. This approach could also eliminate the checks and balances that benefit clients who have financial advisors, accountants, and lawyers working independently of one another on their clients' behalf.

HOW TO READ THE "ALPHABET SOUP"

CFP. A Certified Financial Planner analyzes your personal finances and devises a strategy to help you meet your goals. Unfortunately, anyone can hang out a shingle that says "financial planner." To be considered a professional, however, a planner must have the CFP designation, which is awarded to practitioners who master the following: complete a comprehensive course of study at a university or college, pass a twenty-hour certification exam that covers tax planning, employee benefits, retirement planning, investment management, estate planning, and insurance. Before earning the CFP mark, a planner must also work three years in a kind of apprenticeship, pass an ethics review, and pledge to act with integrity and objectivity. And finally, the planner must take a minimum of thirty hours of continuing education every two years to maintain the certification.

CFA. A Chartered Financial Analyst must demonstrate knowledge of economics, financial accounting, portfolio management, security analysis, and standards of conduct. This is the designation that many Wall Street analysts must have, but that certain financial advisors obtain because they're serious about managing investment portfolios. Candidates must pass a rigorous exam and meet continuing education requirements.

CPA. To become a Certified Public Accountant, an individual must pass a difficult two-day exam and meet continuing education requirements. Most states require a college or postgraduate degree. CPAs provide accounting, tax advisory, personal finance, and business consulting services.

PFS. The Personal Finance Specialist is a CPA who has spent at least 250 hours doing financial planning in each of the previous three years, submitted six references to verify the work experience, and has passed a challenging exam. It is similar to a CFP designation.

CLU. The Chartered Life Underwriter designation is geared for insurance professionals who complete a series of courses through the American College in Bryn Mawr, Pennsylvania.

ChFC. By taking additional courses through the college on comprehensive financial planning, participants can also earn the designation of Chartered Financial Consultant.

RIA. Don't be too impressed by those listing Registered Investment Advisor as their only credential. All it means is that an advisor has filled out a Securities and Exchange Commission form detailing educational and professional experience and paid an annual fee. Having it does not carry an endorsement from the SEC, but almost anyone selling investment securities—stocks, bonds, and mutual funds—must be registered.

ADV. Form ADV, also known as the Uniform Application for Investment Advisor Registration, is a lengthy document filed by registered investment advisors with the U.S. Securities and Exchange Commission. It contains detailed information about the advisor and essential information for anyone looking to hire an investment advisor. Prospective clients should ask an advisor for copies of Form ADV, parts I and II.

Financial Planner as Team Coordinator

As an inheritor, you would probably be grateful to have someone act as your quarterback, helping call the plays for a variety of actions, such as buying life insurance, implementing estate planning, devising investment strategy, and overseeing tax planning. While some people rely on a trusted attorney or CPA to serve in this role, a certified financial planner is often best suited for the job. A financial planner is trained as a generalist, who can refer you to specialists when needed.

In fact, looking for a financial planner is often compared to the chore of trying to find a good doctor. You want one with a good education and training, as well as a pleasant bedside manner. But here's another very important way in which financial planners are like family doctors. They don't always tell you want you want to hear, but rather what you need to know.

Individuals are motivated to see a financial planner when they feel an urgency—such as a life-changing event or receipt of a large lump sum. When inheritors seek out financial advice, they are often looking to invest immediately. But the planner might not see investing as the clients' biggest issue. He might be more concerned about other aspects of their financial lives. Our financial planner, for example, declined to deal with our investment concerns until we had taken steps to protect all our assets by obtaining umbrella insurance and drawing up our estate plans. It's an awful lot like the patient who goes to the doctor complaining of an itching rash, only to be told she really should be more concerned about her high blood pressure.

And while you might be a bit surprised when you leave the planner's office, you also feel peace of mind that the planner has the experience and the knowledge to identify the greatest threats to your financial health. So it was in our case. It was only the urgency we felt to deal with the investments that prodded us to get umbrella insurance and complete estate planning (and even then it took many, many months).

Selecting an advisor might seem like a lot of work, and it can be, but remember, your financial health is at stake. Here's how to select a financial planner:

- Education. More is usually better. Many financial planners have advanced degrees in business and finance as well as an undergraduate degree.
- Accreditation. Anyone can call himself a financial planner. The advisor you choose should be a "certified financial planner," or CFP, who must pass a rigorous exam, meet certain educational and professional requirements, and subscribe to a code of ethics and professional standards to use the CFP designation.
- Experience. A minimum of five years' experience is advisable, though not essential if other qualification are met. Even the best planners have to start somewhere and you might encounter one who's still in her third year of practice.
- Compensation. Determine whether you prefer to pay a fee or a commission, or a combination of the two, for your financial advice. About one in five planners is fee-only, accepting payment only for advice rather than taking commissions on products sold. Most fee-onlies also manage investments for a fee, usually a percentage of assets under management. However, many commission-based planners offer advice for a fee, or provide a combination of fee and commissioned services. Whatever method the planner uses, be sure you understand exactly how and how much you will pay.

TO FEE OR not to fee? Over the years, dozens of readers have asked me for advice on how to pick a financial planner—and most have told me emphatically that they want a fee-only planner. I can certainly understand why. Rather than get paid by commission on investments sold, a fee-only planner is paid for advice, by the hour or by the financial plan. If you go to a planner who is paid by commission, how do you know whether she is choosing investments that are better for you or better for her? What if some of your needs could best be met by commissionless products such as your 401(k) plan or Treasury bonds? Would the planner tell you? As one financial planner who switched from commission to fee-only told me, it was a relief to "sit on the same side of the table" as his clients. Unfortunately, I've seen too many consumers who were sold investments that obviously weren't right for them because they generated high commissions.

Sophisticated (read "affluent") consumers now recognize this potential conflict of interest and seek out fee-only planners. In response, many advisors who get paid by commission offer what's known as fee-based planning in addition to their regular services. If the client prefers, they charge for their advice rather than get paid by commission. Some will offset the cost of their advice if they recommend an investment with a commission. Critics contend, however, that this isn't really fee-only planning.

Some fee-only planners act only as money managers for the wealthy, charging 1 percent or less of the amount under management, say $500,000 or more. But others do charge for advice and financial plans. Hourly advice can range from $75 to as high as $200 and plans can cost from $400 for a quick checkup to $1,000 for a retirement plan to $2,000 or $3,000 or more for a comprehensive plan.

The vast majority of investors, however, still work with

stockbrokers or other commission-based advisors. About 80 percent of financial planners work on commission. Why is this? To some extent, it's just human nature. Deep down, I think many of us would rather be "sold" some products than take the initiative and buy them. And some people cannot afford to pay the up-front cost of fee-only planning. They'll pay commissions—even higher ones over time—as they invest. If you choose to go with a commissioned planner, be certain you understand exactly how and how much he will be paid.

- Personal recommendations. Most people—almost 80 percent according to one recent survey—rely on family, friends, and coworkers to recommend a financial advisor. This can be a good way to begin compiling a list of prospects.
- Referral services. If you can't obtain personal recommendations, call a referral line run by one of the financial planning associations. For a certified financial planner, contact the Financial Planning Association at 800-282-PLAN or *www.fpanet.org*. For a fee-only certified financial planner, contact the National Association of Personal Financial Advisors at 1-888-FEE-ONLY (333-6659).
- Selection. Narrow your choices to three and then call each one. Determine whether the kind of services provided fits your needs. Do you need a planner who works mainly with entrepreneurs or who specializes in dealing with the newly divorced? Also, determine if your income and assets match the planner's client base.

You don't want to be the $50,000 account lost among the million-dollar clients.

- Personal chemistry. Next, meet with three planners you have chosen. Most will offer a free, one-hour get-acquainted session. It's critical that you and the planner hit it off in what could become a very important relationship. Robert N. Veres, the Kennesaw, Georgia, publisher of *Inside Information*, a newsletter for financial advisors, says, "For a financial planning engagement to work, there has to be something more than a business relationship. It's too personal to be impersonal."

- Life planning. Some financial planners are striving to do more than help clients manage their finances. They are employing coaching skills to help them establish their life's goals. This can be a valuable tool for heirs, whose inheritances often force them to rethink their priorities. The coaching method, because it requires clients to be accountable to their coaches, can help them set and reach their goals.

- Disclosure. Ask for a detailed explanation of how the planner is compensated and for a Uniform Application for Investment Advisor, also known as an ADV form. It is important that the planner give you the ADV willingly (part I and II) and that you read it. Most financial planners must file this disclosure form with the federal Securities and Exchange Commission. It contains a treasure trove of information on the advisor's education, background, work history, any disciplinary actions, lawsuits, types of investments usually recommended, relationships, and affiliations with other companies, potential conflicts of interest, and methods of compensation.

- Client referrals. Ask the planner for references from three existing clients, then be sure to call them.
- Implementation. It's important to understand from the outset how much work the planner will do to implement the advice given. A strategy won't do you any good sitting between the covers of a fancy folder. Determine whether you will need to meet quarterly or annually with the advisor. Ask the planner how he or she will deliver the advice. Will it be a lengthy manuscript, in the form of pie charts, or summed up in a letter? Decide which method you prefer.
- Risk tolerance. Make sure the planner understands what level of risk you're willing to take on your investments and act accordingly.
- Teamwork. Inquire how the planner works with other experts, such as attorneys, accountants, and insurance brokers. Beware of people who say they can do everything. Financial services are so complicated nowadays that few people can be experts in all areas.
- Finally, once you've settled on a planner, don't be afraid to keep asking questions about your finances. As you learn more, you'll probably have more sophisticated questions.

The Right Planning Stuff

If you still need help screening for a financial planner, then consider the characteristics that the best in the business share. Mary Rowland, a veteran financial writer and author of *Best Practices for Financial Advisors,* interviewed fifty-five planners from across the country who are regarded by the media and their peers as top-notch. What did they have in common?

- They are excellent listeners.
- They are teachers. Nearly every planner Rowland interviewed had a strong connection to teaching, whether it was teaching children, investors, or other financial advisors. Many said that teaching helped them to learn and to translate what they know to their clients.
- They have excellent communications skills. What good is their knowledge if they can't impart it?
- They don't boast the highest returns. In the beginning of the planning process, Rowland says, clients often think the main function of the advisor is to beat the returns of the S&P 500 stock index. "But in the end, every client would agree that the relationship is what's important to them. The good planners I talked with always ask about your family, your marriage, and your job. These are the things that make the difference between having a good life or not."

Attorneys—We All Need Them

I've used the services of at least six different attorneys to handle everything from noisy neighbors to an injury on the job to estate planning. But I still find the prospect of hiring one intimidating. We've all heard the horror stories of attorneys who did very little and charged a lot. But there are times in our lives when we simply must hire an attorney to help solve a problem or provide a special expertise, such as estate planning. The good news is that the world is full of attorneys. Thanks to competition, we can find one who is knowledgeable and considerate of our needs.

Many inheritors will need to deal with estate planning legalities, both their benefactors' and their own. But whatever you do, don't try this at home! Sure, you can buy books, software, and audiotapes that offer to help you walk through settling an estate or drawing up a living trust. But unless you have no relatives, lead a remarkably uncomplicated life, and don't care who or what gets your money, I'd recommend a good estate planning attorney. You're paying not just for expertise, but for wisdom and professional follow-through.

Here's an example. When we first called on our estate planning attorney to draw up a living trust, he asked us several important questions that hadn't yet occurred to us. Had we picked a guardian for our two young sons? If we should both die before they reached adulthood, did we want them to get their full inheritance at age eighteen or in increments as they reached certain milestones? (See Chapter 13, Planning Your Own Estate.) And was there anybody else who might conceivably depend on us in the future that we should provide for?

That question gave us pause. My husband's parents were then both in their seventies, in failing health, and living on a fixed income. During a recent bad spell, we had helped pay for them to receive Meals on Wheels. We agreed that they might need our help again in the future. So our attorney added to the trust a provision that the successor trustee (should something happen to both of us) could provide support if needed to my husband's parents from our estate, which was ultimately intended for our sons.

The best attorneys are not always the highest-priced ones. Kent Hickey, a financial planner, offers a case in point. He recently worked with a family of several grown children who were to share a $1 million estate. The attorney who wrote the trust offered to settle it for $20,000. Another attorney who didn't specialize in the field quoted $40,000 plus expenses. Finally, the heirs met with one of the leading estate planning attorneys in their area and were impressed with him. "He has done splendid work," Hickey reported. His bill was $10,000.

"Don't hate attorneys," advises Kenneth Moscaret, an attorney and consultant on legal fees. "Learn to get the most out of them." When consumers take their cars in for repairs, they generally get an estimate of the cost before opening their wallets. They're not likely, notes Moscaret, to tell the mechanic: "Just fix whatever you think is wrong and send me the bill." Yet when most people have legal problems, that's how they handle the legal fees, he says.

Increasingly, attorneys expect their savvy clients to ask for an estimate and to request value for their money. In an ideal relationship, the lawyer is a trusted partner and problem solver.

So how do you select an attorney? Referrals are still the best way. Don't expect the first person you ask to have the perfect recommendation. Keep asking. Get referrals from people who've had the same kind of legal problem as you and have similar financial resources. Then interview two or three attorneys. If you are looking for an estate planning attorney, call the trust department of a bank or financial institution with whom you do business (assuming the institution has one). Explain that you're a customer and ask for the names of attorneys with whom the trust department deals on a regular basis.

To gather names of attorneys with certain specialties and information about them, contact your state or local bar association.

Accountants—Beyond Tax Preparation

It may no longer be practical for you to do your taxes on your own or using software once you've received an inheritance. The more complicated your finances are, the more you can benefit from tax planning rather than tax preparation. While there has been much talk in recent years of tax simplification, the tax code has only gotten longer and murkier. For example, your good fortune could push you into the realm of the AMT or Alternative Minimum Tax, a looking-glass tax world that can cost affluent taxpayers thousands in extra income taxes. A good CPA can lessen the bite and devise strategies to reduce your taxes in the future.

How do you select a CPA? Again, use personal referrals. Also, obtain names from state chapters of the American Institute of Certified Public Accountants. Find someone with whom you have rapport and who works with clients like you.

If your finances are only moderately complicated you could use the services of an enrolled agent, who is licensed by the IRS. For more information on enrolled agents contact the National Association of Enrolled Agents at 800-424-4339, *www.naea.org.* Unless your tax situation is quite straightforward, you should probably avoid the services of tax preparers, who are usually seasonal workers.

Appraisers—Valuing the Valuables

If you inherit some valuable jewels from your grandmother, you'll need to know what they're worth so you can insure them. If your parents leave their Asian art collection to you and your two siblings, to be divided equally, you'll need to determine the artifacts' value before you can divvy them up. That's where an impartial expert known as a personal appraiser can help.

As eBay and "Antiques Roadshow" have taught us, those ugly pots in the attic or old cereal boxes in the garage could turn out to be collectibles with substantial value. Choosing a personal property appraiser can be a challenge, however, because the field is essentially unregulated. Using an unqualified appraiser can cost you, unfortunately. A poor appraisal could cause you to sell an item for less than its worth, to over- or underinsure it, reduce your fair share of an inheritance, or put you at risk of being audited by the IRS should you give an item away and claim an excessive tax deduction.

When interviewing appraisers:

- Never hire someone who asks to be paid based on a percentage of the appraised value. This is a glaring conflict of interest that results in overinflated values. Charges should be based on a flat rate, per item, or on an hourly fee.
- Ask appraisers how they would deal with items outside their areas of expertise. Many appraisers specialize. Good ones consult other experts when appropriate.
- Ask what kind of appraisal report you will receive. You should get a typewritten, comprehensive report explaining how the property was valued.
- Remember that sentiment has no value. So even if you know in your heart that your mother's silver collection is special, be prepared to accept a less emotional evaluation.

Your best hope of getting a good appraiser is to seek out one accredited by one or both of two professional organizations—the American Society of Appraisers (800-272-8258, *www.appraisers.org*) and the International Society of Appraisers (202-241-0359).

ARTISTIC APPRECIATION

IF YOU SUSPECT something is valuable, you should check. In my family's case, we had always treasured several paintings that my paternal grandfather, an Ohio English professor, brought back from England in the early 1900s. He had traveled there to learn more about novelist Thomas Hardy and purchased the turn-of-the-century paintings by artist Frederick Whitehead, who specialized in depicting "Hardy Country." The largest, which hung in our living room, showed fisherman throwing their nets into a moonlit river.

I had long thought that the painting might have some value. So, before sending it by moving van to our home in California, I had it appraised. I was fortunate to find a fine art appraiser who belonged to one of the professional societies. She came over to the house, examined the pictures, took photos, and went home to do research. She called later to say that the river scene was worth $8,000, and afterward supplied a detailed written report.

My instincts failed me, however, when it came to the old books at my parents' house. My husband and I were there for only a few days and I couldn't find a book appraiser on short notice. I placed a call to one back in San Diego, but while waiting for a response I decided to start winnowing the collection. I just assumed that the crumbling, mildewed books more than one hundred years old "must" be valuable and carefully set them aside to take home. I was amused at the tawdry 25-cents-apiece detective books from the thirties and forties that my parents had long forgotten. Thinking that I would never read them and they must have no value, I had my husband lug them to a library donation center. As he was driving there, the call came in from the San Diego appraiser. He said he couldn't say much without seeing the books. Okay, I said. But by the way, what about old detective paperbacks? They didn't have any worth, did they?

Actually, some did, he told me, some of them were worth several dollars each, those with original sale prices on the cover of 25 or 35 cents.

I'd just sent my husband to give away a dozen or more like that. When he returned, he gamely offered to go back and un-donate them. But we were short on time. And besides, I thought, maybe some collector would have fun finding a small treasure. Today, however, I do wish I had them, if for no other reason than to see whether they had increased in value.

Therapists for Emotional Issues

If you are depressed you probably can't and you certainly shouldn't be making important financial decisions. It is not uncommon for family members to feel depressed after the death of a loved one. Many organizations, such as hospitals and hospices, offer grief counseling. When the grieving is severe or goes on unabated, say for more than a year, it is probably time to seek additional professional help.

There is a major difference between a psychiatrist and a psychologist. A psychiatrist is a medical doctor who can prescribe antidepressants and other drugs; a psychologist has been trained to help patients solve problems through talk therapy, hypnosis, and other methods. Many people dealing with grief first seek the services of psychologists, who can be more affordable and will try to resolve the problem without drugs. However, some problems associated with grieving, such as depression, anxiety, and sleeplessness, can be helped with medicines. A good psychiatrist will use a combination of medicines and talk therapy. For referrals to a mental health professional, ask your doctor.

Decluttering with Professional Organizers

An inheritance can be a clutter-creating event. Even if you weren't a clutter bug before your inheritance, that could change. You could inherit a house full of stuff, which could become clutter in your house and garage, or you could be so distracted by dealing with the estate that you let your home go, or both. As your parents aged, they might have become too tired or ill to do their annual spring cleaning. If they left you a small landfill of stuff to sort, don't just throw it away. Find a clutter buddy, either a friend or relative, or hire a professional organizer to help you.

Professional organizers can be a great help in integrating the files, financial papers, and photos from the inheritance with your own. Sometimes it's helpful to have someone with a trained eye devise a new and better way to organize. Naturally you're going to want to hire someone you can trust with your valuables and your sensitive personal information. Look for an organizer who is certified by the National Association of Professional Organizers (*www.napo.net*), which requires members to honor a code of ethics. The group also provides referrals by region through an information line at 512-206-0151.

Chapter 12

Children of Affluence

Hey, Daddy! I want a golden goose. Give it to me now!
—Veruca Salt, *Charlie and the Chocolate Factory*

If your inheritance gave your net worth a significant bump up, you will have more options and more decisions to make about how you want to live your life. And some choices to improve your life can create mixed feelings—as purchasing our current house five years after receiving my inheritance did for me. We hadn't meant to spend so much when we first decided to shop for a bigger house, but then we found a house that seemed perfect for us—spacious, quiet, private, and near my children's school and friends. It was a house we could have afforded without an inheritance, given the equity in our old house and our salaries, but the price was high enough that we felt much more comfortable using $100,000 from the inheritance as part of the down payment.

A few weeks before escrow was to close I began to fret

about our children. All the wonderful reasons for picking the house now seemed all wrong. The rolling green lawns in front and back where I had envisioned children gamboling now seemed excessive, as big as a golf course. The walk-in closet in the master bedroom was almost as large as my boys' old bedrooms. This house was twice as large and more than twice as expensive as our first home. And it was a major step up from the kind of two-bedroom home that both my husband and I grew up in. I began to think, This isn't me.

I wondered how we would compare to some of our neighbors and their similarly big homes. These people were obviously really rich, not phony interlopers like us. Would our kids expect us to keep pace with the expensive toys and sports equipment they no doubt bought their children? Finally, I asked my husband, "Aren't you worried about the effect the new home will have on our children? Don't you think they'll become spoiled?" He looked puzzled: "What, are we getting servants?" (His way of telling me to lighten up.)

This kind of fretting over the effect an upgrade in lifestyle could have on kids is quite common, according to Michael Stolper, a San Diego financial consultant to the wealthy, because parents tend to think the way they grew up is the "right way." Thus, the proverbial, "when I was your age, I walked ten miles in the snow" speech. I'll probably forever consider buying a teenager a new car the hallmark of indulgence because I grew up feeling lucky to borrow my parents' used cars, and didn't have my own dilapidated vehicle until I was twenty-three.

Once we moved in, I was thrilled with the house. But the transition from a middle-class neighborhood to an upper-middle-class one was at times discomforting for me. I can remember bringing two of my older son's friends to our new home and cringing when I overheard one tell the other: "Have you seen their new house? It's a mansion!"

My children, of course, quickly processed such comments and came to the inevitable conclusion that we had suddenly become filthy rich. Because they were just ten and six at the time, no amount of explaining could persuade them that our level of wealth was the same as it was at the old house. We had only rearranged what we owned. For the first two years that we lived here, when I refused to buy them something they wanted, my kids came up with what they thought was a killer retort: "If you can afford to buy this house, you can afford to buy me a CD . . . a computer . . . a [fill-in-the-blank]!"

The Gimme Generation

For generations, Americans have hoped, worked, and sacrificed to give their children every opportunity to have a better life than they had. They've scrubbed floors, worked two jobs, did whatever it took to put them through college or provide an opportunity. Call it the "my son/daughter the doctor" syndrome. We are a land built by immigrants seeking better opportunities, an ethos carried on by later generations.

But with the surging affluence of the late twentieth

and early twenty-first centuries, we are at a crossroads. Is more always better? How much is too much? Parents who are comfortable financially now have different worries—that their children won't be as well off as they are and, indeed, will be hindered by the abundance their parents enjoy.

A 1996 Survey of Affluent Americans (defined as the top 1 percent of the population) by U.S. Trust, concluded: "The wealthiest parents in the United States worry about the effects of 'affluenza' on their children—the notion that too much affluence can distort children's values and rob them of initiative. They are concerned that their children have grown up sheltered from the reality that it takes hard work to attain affluence."[1]

BATTLING ENTITLEMENT ATTITUDES

ROCHELLE, WHO WILL soon receive a $200,000 inheritance, lives in an upscale community of Southern California suburban ranchettes, with a backyard pool and Jacuzzi next to the custom home she designed. It's a neighborhood liberally populated with horses and SUVs. Although she enjoys the lifestyle that she and her husband, an engineer, have worked to achieve, Rochelle does worry about her four children's attitudes toward money. They range from thirteen to twenty-four years of age. Rochelle says that society—and she counts herself in this—is too child-centered, too indulgent. She wants her kids to make it on their own in the world. Like many affluent parents, Rochelle has to work at helping them become self-sufficient.

She compares their behavior to hers when she was growing up. When she was the age of her two children who are now in college, says Rochelle, "I would never call home collect. I never would ask my parents for money." But like most children today, hers not only ask for money, but feel entitled to it. She says. "A lot of conflict comes from when we say no."

Not surprisingly, in the last half of the 1990s the affluent were one of the nation's fastest growing economic groups, though the end of the high-tech boom and the 1999–2002 stock market decline took a heavy toll. According to the Spectrem Group, a research and consulting company, affluent households (those with $500,000 net worth excluding principal residence) rose from 2.7 million in 1995 to 13.7 million in 1999 and dropped to 9.6 million in 2001. Even with the hit these households took from the bear market and recession at the turn of the century, their numbers still increased threefold in just six years.[2]

The effect of all this affluence, unfortunately, is to encourage our desire for even more. Juliet B. Schor, author of *The Overspent American*, using a Merck Family Fund poll, found that 27 percent of households with more than $100,000 income say they can't afford to buy everything they need. And one in five of those households say they spend almost all their income on life's basic necessities. These Americans, concludes Schor, live in a state of perpetual material dissatisfaction.[3]

We have always engaged in competitive acquisition, says Schor. This practice accelerated after World War II, as Americans sought to keep up with those infamous neighbors, the Joneses, using possessions to declare their success. Now, however, she says, we no longer feel compelled just to keep up with the Joneses down the street who have roughly the same annual income, but to match the unrealistic living standards of fictional people on television shows or sports and entertainment celebrities. "When twenty-somethings can't afford much more than a utilitarian studio but think they should have a New York apartment to match the ones they see on 'Friends,' " she writes, "they are setting unattainable consumption goals for themselves, with dissatisfaction as a predictable result." Schor's studies led her to a fascinating finding—for every additional hour of television watched per week, a person's spending increases by $218 annually.[4]

A variety of forces, not just TV, make consumerism hard to resist. Though we have many more material things than ever before, we have much higher expectations than previous generations did. Items once considered luxuries, such as dishwashers, microwaves, air conditioners, cable TV, and cell phones, are now deemed necessities. Consequently most Americans don't think of themselves as affluent—even though the average size of a new home has doubled since the 1950s and our roads are clogged with SUVs.

It's little wonder that parents worry about their children's attitude toward money. For the first time in history, say the authors of the book *Affluenza*, children are getting most of their information from marketing campaigns rather than from family, school, or church. "Kids are really targeted," says coauthor John de Graaf. Marketers openly discuss how to increase the "nag factor" on a product and "how to get kids to break through the gate-keeper," the parent. "Marketing to children has become the hottest trend in the advertising world. Children are now used effectively by marketers to influence their parents' purchases of big-ticket items, from luxury automobiles to resort vacations and even homes."

These messages can put considerable pressure on affluent families. After all, the parents have the money to buy many of the products pitched to their children. Invoking the parental veto can be harder if you can't honestly say, "We can't afford it."

THE BABY-SITTER AND TRUST-FUND CLUB

FINANCIAL INSTITUTIONS ARE catching on to the fears of affluent parents about their children's material advantages. Here's how a magazine ad for U.S. Trust begins: " 'Daddy, can I have a trust fund?' 'Not my kids!' you shriek. 'They're just not like that. They grew up baby-sitting and mowing lawns for pocket money. Every summer they sold pizza, waited tables or slaved away in some other job. And the only free ride we gave them was the limo to their prom.' " The ad then goes on to describe how parents can make tax-advantaged transfers of their wealth to their children: "Furthermore, this is something that can be achieved without your children knowing anything about your financial affairs that might dampen their own ambitions or curb their natural potential."

U.S. Trust could pinpoint these attitudes because it has

frequently surveyed the affluent. In 1996[5] nearly 70 percent of affluent parents surveyed said they worried their children would place too much emphasis on material possessions. More than half feared their offspring would be naive about the value of money and how hard it is to earn, would spend beyond their means, and would have their initiative and independence undermined by their material advantages. In addition, more than half worried about making wise inheritance choices for their children.

Depriving Your Kids with Money

So how much money is too much to give your kids? How much stuff is too much stuff for kids to have? Experts agree that "affluenza" is more a state of mind than an income bracket. Janet Bodnar, senior editor at *Kiplinger's Personal Finance* magazine, writes that "no matter what your income, any amount of money can be toxic, if you lavish too much of it on your kids."

Alice B. Reinig, a San Diego psychologist who consults with affluent families, says that almost anyone can spoil a child. All you have to do is "give them what they want, without them having to put out a lot to get it." Saying yes to your child's requests can be the easiest way out at the time. But, she says, "It's a quick fix, as opposed to dealing with the emotions behind the request. They will not have a resource in their pocket when times are hard."

Developing healthy money attitudes in your child is not about whether you buy him the latest Nintendo game or take him on a ski vacation every winter. It's your whole worldview and how well you convey it. I've known wealthy children who were unspoiled, unaffected, and hard working, thanks to their parents. And I've seen kids in families of modest means who rarely felt deprived. The common denominator for both is hands-on parenting and frequent communication of family values.

But, clearly, the more material goods you have and the faster you get them, the less likely you'll be to appreciate any single one of those things. It's only human nature. I had an epiphany about the downside of giving children too much one Christmas when my older son was six. As usual, he had received so many gifts from my husband and myself, his grandparents, and other relatives that he was literally dazed and could not have named all the presents he'd gotten. His friend down the block, however, was one of six children from a religious family who neither expected—nor got—many presents for Christmas. His one gift was a pair of skates and he was clearly delighted. He had been waiting and hoping for them. When I saw him putting his skates on with a big grin, it was at that moment that I realized that you could deprive your children by giving them too much—deprive them of the joy of anticipation, patience, and eventual reward. Now, true, it would be unrealistic to think that my family and I could adopt another family's particular lifestyle. But ever since then, at the holidays, I've often stopped and asked myself whether I'm "depriving" my children by giving them too much.

Challenges of High-End Child-Rearing

Many inheritors were already affluent before they received their bequest (or bequests). Others will be dealing with the special challenges of rearing children in more affluent circumstance for the first time. It is all too easy for the upper middle class and the wealthy to insulate themselves from the children with child-care providers and servants. The result is sometimes neglect and loss of the bond of trust between parent and child. At the same time, children might be expected to live up to parents' high expectations to follow a family dynasty or a particular path to material success. Poor little rich kids can be very poor indeed. Wealth can erode those things that make people happy individuals, such as self-esteem, self-worth, motivation, discipline, trust, and friendship. All in all, says wealth consultant John Levy, this can be a "pretty discouraging picture."

The solution, of course, is good parenting combined with a clear expression of parental values. Levy says that many wealthy parents worry that money will make their kids lazy. But if the parents have done a good job of parenting, he says, that won't happen. If the parents enjoy their work and feel that it is important, this value will transfer to their children.

Here's how to inoculate against "affluenza":

- Good child rearing is important. Parents must spend time loving, nurturing, and teaching their children through the different stages of childhood and adolescence, says Levy. Affluent parents in particular must help their children learn to overcome frustration and pain because of delays and disappointments, and to persevere rather than quit when things aren't going well.

"If they have not learned to earn things, they can feel entitled," says Reinig. "They don't appreciate people and things. It's important for children to anticipate having something." Parents need to be mindful to set a good example in this, because children simply won't buy the philosophy of "Do as I say, not as I do."

• Pick child-care helpers with care. While they should avoid delegating too much parental authority to household helpers, parents must honestly acknowledge that such employees can have a significant impact on the development of their children, says Levy. They should monitor the relationship closely, and not just look out for potentially harmful experiences. They should take into account that children might be attached to an employee and act with sensitivity when the relationship must end. Finally, says Levy, how the parents treat the helpers will, for better or worse, serve as a model for the children in their dealings with future employees and others from economic classes different than their own.

• Teach your children well. Set positive examples by talk and by action. "In my research," says Levy, "it has been remarkable how few inheritors feel that their parents really did this for them." Those who did the best talked about money with their kids. If the subject is avoided, like sex, it becomes something dark and shameful. As children grow, they need to know where their parents' money comes from, how much there is, and what they can expect to receive. They need to see how money is used in their family. Parents should also discuss good and bad financial practices of other families, as well as ethical issues.

"The only long-lasting treatment is to immunize kids against 'affluenza,' starting with small doses of financial education when they're preschoolers and boosting the dosage as they get older," says Bodnar. Unfortunately, many parents do just the opposite. Because they fear their kids won't have incentive, they simply don't talk about money. That only deepens the mystery. If you have qualms about talking money with your kids, remember they will eventually have to manage it on their own. Better to start now with some help from you. Bodnar recommends answering your children's questions forthrightly and in age-appropriate way. And don't tell them more than they need or want to know.

My many attempts to talk candidly with my children usually seem to go well. But I do occasionally overload them with more than they can handle. When my younger son was in second grade, he badgered me to know how much our new house cost, and I told him, figuring he would forget in an hour. The figure $500,000 was meaningless to him. But the next day he told everyone at school it cost $5 million! Sometimes when I go to the ATM, my children inquire how much is in the account. After years of sidestepping the issue, I finally said my checking account contained $2,000. They were angry and felt betrayed that I wasn't using it for something important like Pez collecting or video games. "You have *lots* of money!" they screamed. They turned a deaf ear to my replies that we needed the money to pay the mortgage, insurance, or to get groceries. With any luck—and a few hundred more conversations like that—we'll come to an understanding.

· Set limits. Families who are well off can't always employ the age-old parental standby "we can't afford it" when their children ask to buy something. You'll have to develop your own terminology for such occasions. You might say that the item isn't in your budget—and let them learn what a budget is by receiving a weekly allowance. Or you might have a discussion about "wants" versus "needs." When asked to buy something you consider frivolous, you can say, "No, that's a want, not a need. If you really want it, use your allowance." And stick to your guns. If your kids are like mine, they know how to push your buttons. If you feel guilty about not spending time with them or discomfort over denying them something they want, they can sense it and will be tempted to use your weakness to their advantage.

SCOOPING UP FISCAL RESPONSIBILITY

WHEN VALERIE JACOBS'S son turned sixteen, he didn't receive a new car like some of the kids at his school. Instead, he got permission to drive the family's eight-year-old

Plymouth Voyager minivan. "We told him from the very beginning he was not getting a new car," says Jacobs. And if he wanted a car of his own, he'd have to help pay for it. There's nothing unusual in this scenario, except that Jacobs and her husband could easily afford to make the purchase.

Thanks to a gift of stock in her father's engineering company years ago, Jacobs is worth millions. She is also a psychologist and wealth counselor who consults on the effects of wealth on people's lives. One thing she's sure of: "The wealth itself is not what makes or breaks a person's family." It's the family attitude. And Jacobs intends to foster healthy money attitudes with her two children.

She and her husband encouraged their son to get a job while in high school—first at a Baskin Robbins ice cream shop and then at a steakhouse parking cars. Jacobs had told him if he wanted to travel after college, he'd have to work to pay part of the cost. She thinks some of their talk about self-reliance is catching on with her son and daughter. "They do look at other people and say, 'How spoiled.'"

- Have them manage money now. Most parents would never let a teenager get behind the wheel of a car without taking lessons, getting some practice, and earning a driver's license. Yet these same parents might send their kids off to college or to live on their own without the necessary money skills. It is critical to give children, starting at about age seven, an allowance that need not necessarily be tied to chores. The point of an allowance is not pay for work, but money management. Better to learn their lessons about blowing money on Nintendo and Barbies than when they're tooling off to college with credit card in hand. For more in-depth learning, have your preteens and teens meet with a financial planner to discuss investing. If your child is interested, consider an investment club for teens.

WHEN 2 + 2 = SATISFACTION

DESPITE THE MANY benefits of managing an allowance, only about half the nation's children receive one, according to a 1995 survey by *Zillions*, an online publication of *Consumer Reports*. Interestingly, the other half ended up with about the same amount of money each week, the survey showed, but they got it piecemeal through parental handouts. The two groups, however, reported distinctly different levels of satisfaction about what they got. Those who had a set weekly allowance were happier than those who didn't. The allowance-less set were more likely to go broke each week and less inclined to save.

- Assign children responsibilities. Children need to develop a sense of competency and self-sufficiency. Encourage this by having them help around the house—setting the table, taking out the trash, or helping with a pet. In high school, they can build on this by working at a summer job. Ideally, says Levy, the children should find the jobs on their own, without the parents' help.
- Don't send mixed messages. You can't indulge your child with material things while she is very young, then suddenly throw her into austere circumstances to teach her about the real world. Not only is this unkind,

you're setting her up for failure and resentment. The
lifestyle you want for your child should be the one
you're living now.

· Give them a sense of heritage. Like all other children,
the affluent need a sense of family pride. They need to
feel good about who made the family money and how
they managed it, says Levy. Give them an admirable
tradition to uphold. Children love to hear stories about
their ancestors, and all the better if they can trace the
relative's work to their life today. My two sons love to
hear the Go Fish story, about how my grandmother as
a widow worked for Compton's Encyclopedia by day
and created children's games in her free time. I tell
them she wasn't a traditional grandmother—you were
more likely to find her with a martini in her hand than
a rolling pin, but that not many people can claim an
entrepreneurial granny.

If the money inherited came from undesirable activities, advises Levy, be honest and share a clear commitment to use the money in socially responsible ways.

· Choose schools with care. Affluent families have many
options when it comes to sending children to school—
public or private, even local or boarding school.
Selecting a school involves so many variables, from the
child's personality to the quality of neighborhood
schools, that there is no one right answer, says Levy. The
majority of affluent Americans, according to the U.S.
Trust survey, send their children to public elementary
and secondary schools. About 70 percent plan to pay for
their children to attend private undergraduate college.

- Plan your estate with care. Over and above all the tax and legal considerations, Levy recommends a few guiding principles. First, the "parents' distribution of their wealth among their children must be fair to all," he says. Also, inheritors should be kept informed and "their wishes should be heard and considered." And finally don't use the threat of disinheritance to manipulate behavior. There's danger in trying to force a child to deny his true nature, and says Levy, "It's almost always destructive." Requiring that a grown child attend a particular college or work in the family business against his desires might work for a few years, but the anger and resentment is bound to take its toll on family relations eventually.

- Career choices can be difficult for children of successful parents. If a parent is especially successful, following the same career path can be painful and unrewarding, says Levy. It's important for affluent young people to find work where they will not be identified as different and where they will have a chance to succeed on their own merits. Those offspring who are most fulfilled, says Levy, have proven they are competent and worthwhile and don't need the family money to lead successful lives.

- Children should be taught about charity at an early age. Giving can be an antidote to many problems associated with inheritance. "Parents and grandparents can seed the thought of sharing by modeling it themselves," says Peg Eddy, a financial planner who works with family-owned businesses. She and her husband, Bob, started when their two sons, now grown, were in grade school. The boys were allowed to pick a charity and the Eddys would send a check in their names. They would also adopt a family at the holidays through their church, select the gifts and food, and deliver them to the family. One year the whole family volunteered to clean up a concourse after the homeless had stayed there for Christmas. "We all pushed brooms and boxed clothes for six hours, got blisters, and were so exhilarated that we had helped," says Eddy.

As they got into high school, the boys took on charitable causes, such as clothes and food drives. Both sons, now in their twenties, continue to do volunteer work. The Eddys also plan to set up a $1,000 scholarship in each son's name at their high school—with the hope that that their sons will contribute when they're able.

Money Can Buy Me Dance Lessons

Of course, being affluent does have its advantages. "Wealthy individuals enjoy a special degree of empowerment," says Paul G. Schervish, director of the Social Welfare Research Institute at Boston College. He divides the kinds of empowerment into three types: spatial, that is the ability to build physical and social barriers around themselves; temporal, the ability to reconstruct the past and bring the future under the control of the present; and psychological, the ability to insulate oneself from the mundane. These descriptions make me think of someone flying in his private jet—physically and socially above everyone else, shaping his future by getting to his destination earlier than he would have on a commercial jet and not having to deal with the mundane task of waiting in long lines for baggage check. And what do we want for our children in life? Something special, certainly not the mundane.

We tend to believe that money can buy for our children what we think of as the better things in life, such as music, dance, and sports lessons, summer camps, overseas travel, and computers. Who wouldn't want these things for their children? I've certainly used our money to pay for these kinds of activities (though sometimes running the risk of overbooking). One researcher I spoke with about inheritance told me he wouldn't accept money from his wealthy mother-in-law because he didn't want to feel controlled, but he would take it on behalf of his teenage son. He wanted the son to have the benefits of an enhanced education and the opportunity to travel.

While parents might place a great deal of importance on these enrichments, at heart they know these will not "make or break" their kids when they go out in the world. When affluent baby boomers were asked in a 1999 U.S. Trust Survey what traits were required for the twenty-first century, 90 percent ranked ambition and willingness to work hard as the most important. And which trait rated last? Coming from a well-to-do family.

Chapter 13

Planning Your Own Estate

I'm not afraid of death. I just don't want to be there when it happens.
—Woody Allen

Now that you've received an inheritance, you no doubt see the value in doing proper estate planning or the harm in poor planning. It's your turn now. All adults need some kind of estate plan, and with what you've inherited, you now have more to protect and pass on to your loved ones. Your family members want to be left with clear instructions and a sense of being treated fairly, not with the chore of sorting through a big mess. If you want your beneficiaries to be grateful, not just for the material goods you leave them, but for your gracious leave-taking, treat them as you would like to be treated. Share your thoughts on your estate openly with them, manage their expectations, avoid surprises, and make your wishes clear. A friend of mine who's had to deal with three estates of family members in recent years, put it succinctly: "Get a good lawyer. Decide who gets what. Then tell them."

Unfortunately, for the past several decades, much of estate planning has been focused on the avoidance of federal estate taxes. In fact, only two out of every one hundred estates has had to pay this hefty tax in recent years. Although the tax affects only the wealthiest Americans, fear of it has driven many to seek professional help in setting up elaborate trusts and charitable gifts to ensure the government is cut out.

The estate tax should not be confused with what are known as death taxes and inheritance taxes. These are levied by some but not all the states and vary from one state to another. It is the federal tax, however, that has proven the most costly and worrisome. Thanks to major tax reform in 2001, the estate tax is diminishing and could disappear altogether in 2010 (or not, read on for an explanation).

Even if the estate tax is abolished, however, there are other compelling reasons to have an estate plan. As an inheritor, you're probably familiar with at least one of these. An estate plan can help:

- Leave your assets to the family members, friends, and charities that you choose
- Provide for young children by naming a guardian and trustee for their finances
- Avoid the hassle and cost of legal proceedings, namely probate
- Prevent family conflict
- Name a trusted person or persons to care for your

health and your finances should you become incapacitated.

If you don't name your beneficiaries, the law of your state will. That could mean that all of your estate goes to the brother you've always loathed and none to your favorite charity that helps children learn to read. "Whatever planning you do is probably better than leaving the choice to chance," says attorney Melitta Fleck.

A Will: The First Step

At the very least, everyone should have a will—a legal document that names the people and organizations you want to inherit your assets. In this document, if necessary, you should also nominate a guardian to care for your children under the age of eighteen (see more on this below). In addition, you should choose an executor, who will manage and distribute the assets in your estate.

A will need not be complicated or costly. But it's a good idea to have an estate planning attorney either prepare it or review it.

For a greater degree of control and flexibility over their estates, many people choose to use trusts. There is more work and greater cost involved, but trusts can perform a variety of jobs. Here are just some of the different types:

- Bypass trust. Intended to reduce or eliminate estate taxes, a common form is the "A–B" trust or marital life estate trust. In non–community property states each spouse has an individual trust. It is typically used by couples whose combined estate could be subject to estate taxes.

- Special needs trust. This trust is usually set up by parents to provide for a child who has serious physical or emotional problems and will need lifetime care. This should be drafted carefully to ensure the continuity of any government assistance, and a trustee must be chosen with great care.
- Charitable remainder trust. With this kind of trust, donors make an irrevocable gift of property such as stock or real estate to a charity or charities. In exchange, donors or other named beneficiaries can receive income for life and an income tax write-off.

IS THIS THE WAY TO REWARD HEIRS?

THE HOTTEST THING to come down the estate planning pipeline in recent years is a controversial legal device known as a "family incentive trust." Popular with the 1990s first-generation wealthy who worried about spoiling their kids, these trusts are designed to dole out money as beneficiaries achieve certain milestones—such as graduating from college, earning an advanced degree, getting married, and having children. While trusts have traditionally parceled out money to young inheritors incrementally as they matured, these designer trusts can have enough strings attached to make any inheritor feel like a puppet. Depending on the creators' strongly held values, incentive trusts have refused to pay out to heirs who had credit card debt, didn't practice the right religion, or didn't do service work. Conceivably a prospective heir could be punished for being gay (and not getting married) or being an entrepreneur and skipping college.

Critics say the impulse might be admirable, but that setting inflexible conditions is no substitute for good parenting. These trusts can reflect the egoism of the creators—the goals that must be met often read like a parent's biography. Wealth consultant John Levy calls incentive trusts an abomination: "It's a very sneaky way of trying to control their children and also force them to be like them. It's a form of bribery." Levy says that such rigid trusts encourage dishonesty because children tend to lie to get what they want. Implicit in the decision to place the restrictions, says Levy, is a "belief that the only thing in life worth working for is making money."

One common and more widely accepted reason for employing trusts, however, is to ensure that children do not receive their entire inheritance at age eighteen or twenty-one. With a trust, parents can stagger the ages at which children receive partial bequests—say twenty-one, thirty, and forty. "Rarely is an eighteen-year-old ready," says attorney Russell Griffith. "I recommend giving them at least two or three opportunities to mess up." Parents should name a trustee to manage the trust funds, either an individual, an institution, or both. The trustee could have the discretion to distribute some or all of the funds sooner than the designated ages for such needs as health, education, maintenance, and support.

Even with more complicated estate plans like trusts, it

is best to have a backup or a simple will that provides for any property inadvertently left out.

Beth, a married forty-one-year-old Midwestern tele-communications manager, inherited $250,000 from her grandfather in four five-year increments ending when she was thirty-five. She thinks the installment approach worked well and allowed her and her husband to get accustomed to handling larger sums of money. "Although it was a stunning amount of money for us, it wasn't nearly enough to change our lives forever," she says. "It forced a little more discipline." By the time she got the last portion, she no longer had the desire to spend it. "It just felt like set-aside money, retirement money."

Choosing a Guardian

When parents name a guardian for their young children in their wills, they should realize they are making a nomination to a court. Most courts try to respect the parental wishes, but there could be circumstances, such as the death or disability of the designated guardian, that render the parents' choice invalid.

Parents also need to designate a responsible person or trustee to manage the money that is left to the children. The guardian and the trustee can be the same person. However, a guardian who is a loving caregiver is not always the best at handling money, so an independent trustee could be necessary. Some attorneys feel that having a trustee dispense money to the guardian can be unnecessarily cumbersome, while others feel the arrangement provides accountability.

Many parents find the selection of a guardian to be an agonizingly difficult task. In fact, it can be a major impediment to completing an estate plan. Not surprisingly, couples sometimes disagree on whom to chose for this important job—his brother, her mother, and 'round it goes. Sometimes people talk back and forth until their youngest child reaches eighteen, then do their estate planning. In some cases, friends or neighbors are better qualified than relatives. And sometimes, you simply have to accept that there is no one perfect choice.

I know one financial planner and his wife—middle-of-the-road Presbyterians—who strongly considered naming family friends because his only brother led such a different life from theirs. The brother was gay and a practicing Buddhist. But the planner finally decided that despite the contrasting lifestyle, his brother would provide the most loving home.

It's also a good idea to authorize the trustee (or the guardian if the same person) to designate money for the guardian's added costs in caring for the children. This can include a lump sum to help in remodeling an existing home or buying a larger one.

Parents might want to include a letter to the guardian conveying their wishes for their children, such as having them take piano lessons, practice a certain religion, or attend a particular college. Parents should review their choice of guardian often, because relationships and circumstances can change. The close friends who lived next door and seemed perfect four years ago may have divorced and moved away.

Avoiding Probate

Just as many people want to avoid having their estates taxed, many would also like to keep their beneficiaries out of probate court. Probate is the legal process of settling a deceased person's estate in local court. The court has all property inventoried and appraised, pays off debts, and then distributes the proceeds to the beneficiaries.

In some states, probate is a fairly benign procedure. But in California, where I live, probate can drag on for months and years and, depending on the size of the estate, end up costing thousands of dollars. Most of the money is usually paid to probate attorneys and executors. Some consumer advocates, like the legal do-it-yourself publishing firm Nolo don't have much good to say about probate. "The system," according to Nolo's *Plan Your Estate*, "usually amounts to a lot of time-wasting, expensive mumbo-jumbo of use to no one but the lawyers involved."

So how can you ensure that your heirs don't end up in probate court? Those with small estates are exempt (the size varies from state to state). Just having a will does not prevent probate. The best means is to create a living trust. This is an extremely flexible legal document that controls the property you transfer into it. When you die, your beneficiaries receive the property—and avoid probate.

It is also possible to arrange for at least some of your property to go directly to your beneficiaries without making a stop at probate court:

- Life insurance proceeds, while generally counted as part of your estate, pass directly to your beneficiaries.
- Retirement accounts, such as 401(k)s and IRAs, go to the beneficiaries as designated on the account documents.
- Transfer-on-death bank accounts. These accounts, which are restricted to cash and government securities, are easy to set up and pass immediately to the designated beneficiary.
- Transfer-on-death securities registration. You can name your beneficiary on a form with a brokerage house, but this method is not available in every state.

Keeping the Peace

If saving money for your heirs doesn't motivate you, then plan your estate in consideration of their feelings. They need to know you remember them. Find out what your heirs want, what would be meaningful to them. "If people don't do estate plans it can create substantial conflicts within the family," says James Miller, a San Diego estate planning attorney. "People fight about Uncle Harry's pot. That stuff creates lasting bitter feelings." Do an inventory—on computer. Make one copy for yourself, and keep one outside the house and one with someone trusted.

Incapacity Happens

By doing estate planning, we are preparing for the eventuality of our deaths. This is also a good time to acknowledge and prepare for the possibility of our incapacity. As discussed in Chapter 2, Planning Together, you don't have to be old to become unable to care for your health or your finances. A serious car accident or a sudden illness can render a healthy fifty-year-old temporarily incapacitated.

All adults should have:

- A durable power of attorney for financial matters. With this document, you authorize a trusted family member or friend to take care of a wide range of financial obligations, from paying bills to making estate plans. Many living trusts provide for the successor trustee to fill this role.
- A durable power of attorney for health care. You name a trusted person to manage your health care should you become incapacitated. This individual should be skilled at communicating with medical staff and making decisions in your best interest.
- A living will or directive to physicians. This document allows you to direct how you want to be cared for in certain situations—whether you would want to be on an artificial breathing machine or to have the artificial administration of food and water, and under what circumstances.

IN OUR TRUST WE TRUST

I WISH I could be more specific in describing the best way to plan an estate. But unfortunately, widely divergent personal situations and different laws from state to state make it impossible. I can tell you, however, that my husband and I worked with an experienced attorney to set up a living trust, whose main purpose was to provide for our two sons, who are now sixteen and twelve, by leaving them all our property—in portions at ages thirty, thirty-five, and forty.

At the time we created the trust, estate taxes kicked in at $600,000 per person, or $1.2 million for our combined estate. Our assets combined with life insurance put us a bit over the mark. Now, with the individual exemption at $1 million (or $2 million combined), and due to increase in coming years, we should be fine. Although the estate tax might be eliminated in the future, for now we still need the bypass trust to use both credits and to avoid the cost and hassle of probate.

The cost of creating a trust like this (it runs to twenty-six pages and tries to cover every conceivable eventuality) and related supportive documents is likely to be $2,000 to $3,000. One of the biggest chores in creating a living trust is to retitle all your major assets in the name of the trustee: brokerage accounts, bank accounts, anything of value. A good attorney will take care of transferring your real estate. I have to admit it seems pretentious to get the property tax bill addressed to us as trustees of the Perry Family Trust. What next? A drawbridge? A coat of arms?

The Uncertain State of the Estate Tax

As part of his 2000 election campaign, President George W. Bush promised to repeal it the federal estate tax. And, indeed, estate tax reform was a major part of the huge tax package known as the Economic Growth and Tax Relief Reconciliation Act of 2001. What finally emerged after the legislative back-and-forth, however, stretches the limits of the meaning of the word "repeal."

Will there be an estate tax in the future?

The answer is a definite yes, no, maybe so. The tax was to phase out starting in 2002, until it disappears altogether in the year 2010—for that year only. Then, to conform with budget requirements, it is reinstated in 2011 at roughly the same levels as in 2002.

At the time the act was passed in 2001, an estate was exempt from federal taxes if it was below $675,000. Above that threshold estates could be taxed as much as 55 percent. Starting in 2002, the exemption levels began to increase and the maximum tax rate to decrease. Here's how the phaseout is supposed to work:

Year	Exemption	Highest Tax Rate
2002	$1 million	50%
2003	$1 million	49%
2004	$1.5 million	48%
2005	$1.5 million	47%
2006	$2 million	46%
2007	$2 million	45%
2008	$2 million	45%
2009	$3.5 million	45%
2010	repealed	0%
2011	$1 million	55%

This on-again, off-again, on-again estate tax has left many people puzzled and prompted a fair number of jokes about the need for the ultrawealthy to watch their backs in the year 2010. "It's introduced more uncertainty than we've ever had before," says CPA Richard J. Muscio. "Everybody's trying to predict when they're going to pass away. We never used to worry about whether someone was going to live three years or twenty."

Some clients feel confident they'll make it to 2010, says Muscio, and don't want to bother about the other years. Others act as if the tax won't come back in 2011. But that's not prudent, says attorney James Lauth. "For all but 365 days, there is an estate tax. Unless someone is absolutely certain they're going to die in 2010, we've got to plan for an estate tax."

There's also a very real chance that the law will be modified before the repeal arrives. The time between the bill's passage in 2001 and 2010 is "a near-eternity in the universe of tax legislation, and any number of reasons might cause Congress to slow or halt the progress toward total repeal along the way," says Bruno Graziano, an attorney with CCH, the tax and business publisher. While there have been many attempts to eliminate the estate tax, it has been a source of revenue to the federal government since 1916.

In the meantime, anyone with existing estate documents should review them to make certain the 2001 law does not create problems. Attorneys report that some poorly drafted living trusts refer specifically to an older $600,000 threshold, which could leave assets to unintended recipients and send heirs scrambling. In other instances, trusts worded in certain ways and written under previous rules could disinherit some heirs and overendow others. For example, if a man who has remarried wants to provide for both his second wife and his two children by his first marriage, the trust could be worded in such a way that his children get everything and his wife gets nothing—or vice versa.

In addition to raising the threshold for taxing estates, the legislation also:

- Changed the state "pickup" tax. Many states impose death taxes on estates that owe federal tax. The state tax is taken out of what is owed to the IRS. So there is no extra tax to the estate and the federal government counts the state death tax as a credit. Starting in 2002, the credit amount has been reduced. As a result, in some high tax states like New York, New Jersey, and Connecticut, the tax burden for larger estates could actually remain high despite the reduction in federal estate tax.

- Opened the door to a new way of calculating basis. Currently, when individuals inherit assets, those assets receive what is known as a "step-up in basis" from what the deceased paid for them to their current values. That reduces or eliminates capital gains taxes when the assets are sold. But in 2010 when the estate tax is eliminated, the law would restrict this tax break for the wealthiest Americans—to assets below $1.3 million.

Assets above $1.3 million would receive no step-up in basis.

It could create an accounting nightmare for inheritors. "What's the cost basis of a one-hundred-year-old coin collection?" asks Muscio. "You've got to pay attention to which properties have step-up and which don't. Two pieces of property left to two heirs could have a gross disparity."

For now, Americans with large estates will have to rely on some tried and true methods of reducing their estates. These include:

- Family limited partnerships. Under this increasingly popular scenario, a couple worth several million could set up a partnership in which they are the general partners and their children are the limited partners. Each year they could give their children an ever-larger interest, while maintaining control. Because the heirs don't have legal control of the assets, thus reducing the value, the parents' share could be discounted by 30 to 50 percent for estate tax purposes, subject to approval of the IRS.
- Life insurance. With this method, life insurance is held outside the estate in a nonrevocable life insurance trust and the proceeds would be used to defray estate taxes owed. This works well to keep intact nonliquid assets such as real estate and family businesses.
- Charitable giving. Gifts to charity are deductible for income tax purposes and also have the effect, of course,

of reducing an estate. A variety of estate planning tools can set up donations to charity and provide tax-favorable results.

- Annual gifting. Individuals can give away up to $11,000 each to any other individual or noncharitable institution per year without triggering a gift tax.

Chapter 14

Heir and Share

Money is like muck, not good except it be spread.
—Francis Bacon

I f want to share your estate, you don't have to wait until you're on your deathbed to do so. You can, of course, make gifts to family and friends while you're around to enjoy watching how it's spent. This is known as an "inter vivos" gift or transfer between the living. The transfer can take many different forms—such as when parents underwrite a college education or professional degree for their children, give them seed money to start a business, or help make the down payment on a first house.

These gifts, if made wisely, can grow to be worth far more than the original presents. Higher education can pay huge dividends, in the form of a higher standard of living and better quality of life. And buying a house, though it's a financial challenge initially, is for many people a gateway to financial security, because of the many tax breaks, equity appreciation, and personal stability it provides.

When my mother shared the Go Fish game royalties that she had inherited to help buy our first house, she was making an inter vivos gift, as she was when she had me buy some government bonds on behalf of my children for their prospective college educations. This type of living bequest has been carried out by the rich for years. As Peg Eddy, family business advisor, notes, "The wealthy plan for three generations, not just one."

Generation Tripping

This practice, however, is likely to become more common among the middle class as the baby boomers inherit from their parents. Expect to hear more about "intergenerational" and "multigenerational" financial planning in the coming years—due to the size of the early-twenty-first-century wealth transfer and the growing democratization of financial products and information. Over the past three decades, the vast U.S. middle class has gained access to professional stock management through mutual funds, detailed financial information from the Internet, and quality financial advice through affordable providers like financial planners.

Carol Akright, financial planner and author of *Funding Your Dreams Generation to Generation: Intergenerational Financial Planning to Ensure Your Family's Health, Wealth, and Personal Values*, writes that, "Money is a family resource that can be shared in ways that might help you and other family members fulfill dreams."

She suggests that perhaps it's not best to have each generation stockpile assets, parceling them out occasionally through a lifetime, and finally passing most of them on after death. Akright defines intergenerational financial planning as the use of financial strategies—and communication techniques—to provide continuity, prosperity, and security from generation to generation. You don't have to be wealthy to appreciate that it's hard to work and save money, Akright says, yet it only takes a few simple steps to invest money and make it grow.

Of course, money is not the end in itself. It is a means to an end. Among the dreams that can be funded with help from intergenerational planning are having an interesting career, educating your children, paying off your mortgage before retirement, helping your parents as they age, and being financially independent during retirement.

Another author who promotes the concept of multigenerational strategies is Kevin McKinley, an Eau Claire, Wisconsin, certified financial planner. His book is entitled *Make Your Kid a Millionaire: Eleven Easy Ways Anyone Can Secure a Child's Future.* Don't be fooled by the book's title; it's not just about making your child rich. McKinley points out that saving and investing on behalf of your children can in the end give them much more than money. A better education, for example, gives your offspring more knowledge, more choices, and the means to manage their lives better. If you practice multigenerational planning, you will also give your children a wonderful role model for managing and sharing money.

Families now have great incentives to save and invest for future generations, thanks to recent substantive changes in the tax code. New and improved tax breaks encourage Americans to save for their retirement, for their children's college education, and even for their children's retirement.

Consider the Roth IRA, the new star performer for intergenerational savers. If you're a parent who starts a Roth IRA to save for your own retirement, you can under certain circumstances withdraw contributions from your account to pay for your daughter's college education. If you're older than 59½ you can withdraw both contributions and earnings to fund college. Or you could contribute to the down payment on your son's first home (up to $10,000). If, instead, you let the account grow (because unlike traditional IRAs, with a Roth there are no mandatory distributions), it can eventually pass to your beneficiaries free of income tax. Remember that when you opt to make a contribution to a Roth IRA, you are paying in after-tax dollars. Thus, you don't get a tax deduction. In return, you get a great benefit. You pay no income taxes when you withdraw the money in your retirement. The same is true for your beneficiaries. They can enjoy the tax-free accumulation of your investments and pay no income tax when they take the money out (though there might be estate tax if your estate exceeds the limit). But all in all, it's one heck of deal.

Here's how you might want to share your inheritance using recently enhanced tax breaks:

- Gifting. Under current federal tax law, you can give as much as $11,000 each to as many different people as you like in one calendar year. If you give more than that amount to any one person, you won't necessarily owe gift taxes, but you have to file a form with the IRS. The amount in excess of $11,000 per person is essentially deducted from your lifetime estate tax exemption. Each of us can give away a certain amount of money, at present $1 million, free of estate taxes. We can either pass it along tax free in our estate when we die, or we can use up all or part of the exemption during our lives.

  For maximum effect, you can bunch up gifts. If you want to give your daughter a house down payment, give her $11,000 in late December, then gift her again in early January. If you're married, you and your spouse can each give, bringing the total up to $44,000 in just a few weeks.

  What happens if you want to give more than the limit? Let's say you want to give your son $60,000 one year to start a business. You've given $49,000 more than the annual exclusion. That amount is subtracted (because you've filed the requisite tax form) from your $1 million lifetime exemption. No taxes will be due until you use up all of your exemption.

  Giving away some of your estate, assuming you are financially secure, can be a smart tax move. It should benefit your heirs both now and later. Because gifting decreases the size of your estate and allows assets to grow outside your estate, it could reduce or eliminate any estate taxes when you finally pass it on to your beneficiaries. And it allows them to live better while you are still around to see them enjoy it.

- IRAs. Parents and grandparents can use their Individual Retirement Accounts to harness the power of tax-enhanced compounding for their offspring. While this approach works well with the old-fashioned deductible IRAs (where you get a tax break for your contribution, but have to pay taxes on your withdrawals), it's the Roth IRA with its tax-free withdrawals that can be a bonanza for you and your descendants. Unlike a traditional IRA, a Roth does not require the original owner to make minimum withdrawals. And with both traditional and Roth IRAs, when you leave an IRA to younger beneficiaries, they are allowed to take distributions based on their longer life expectancies—in short, more time for most of the money to compound without paying taxes. Welcome to the "stretch" IRA.

   Here's how it works, according to McKinley: If you put just $2,000 into a Roth today, make no further contributions, and pass away fifty years later, the IRA will have grown to almost $235,000 (assuming a 10 percent return). If you leave it to your daughter, who has a thirty-year post-inheritance life expectancy, she will have to withdraw only $9,300 the first year. And over the next thirty years, she will receive checks to-

taling more than $1 million dollars. If you leave this to
a grandchild instead, the ultimate value of the account
during his lifetime could be tens of millions of dollars.

Even with a non-Roth, the results are not too
shabby. For example, says McKinley, if you are now age
seventy and have a traditional IRA worth $100,000,
earning 10 percent annually, upon your death ten years
later it would be worth $180,000. Should you leave it
to your ten-year-old grandson (who you pray decides
not to blow it all at age eighteen), he could receive distributions of about $2 million throughout his life and
still have $3.6 million left in the account when he turns
sixty-five.

· Kick-start an IRA. Want to maximize the money you
give to your children or grandchildren? As soon as
they're old enough to start earning money—by mowing lawns, baby-sitting, or working at the neighborhood ice-cream shop—help them set up a Roth IRA
account. All they need to get started is actual earned
income—savings or investments don't count.

Then, somewhat like a corporate employer, you
"match" their earnings. With teens, it's probably best
to let them keep most or all of what they make, while
you contribute the equivalent of their earned income
to the account (up to $3,000 in years 2003–2004,
$4,000 in years 2005–2007, and $5,000 starting in year
2008). As they get older you can match what they contribute using whatever formula you prefer.

The beauty of starting that early, assuming your offspring don't dip into the account, is the compounding

over time. For example, if you help your granddaughter invest $3,000 in a Roth IRA starting when she's fourteen and she continues to contribute that amount to the account, which earns 10 percent annually, she'll have $4.2 million at age sixty-five—tax free. Not bad for someone who started out scooping ice cream.

• College savings, or 529, plans. Say good-bye to that old standby, the custodial account (commonly called UTMA or UGMA accounts after the Uniform Transfers/Gifts to Minors Act) that let you save for your children in their names. If you want to set up a college fund for your children or grandchildren, the relatively new state college savings plans are the ticket.

Named for a section of the tax code, 529s allow families of any means to contribute as little as $25 or, in some states, as much as $250,000 to investment accounts overseen by individual states and managed by investment companies such as Vanguard and TIAA-CREF. Anyone—family or friends—can establish an account, but control of the account remains with the account owner, typically a parent or grandparent. And if one child in the family decides to skip college, the account can be used for the benefit of a variety of other family members, including siblings, cousins, even the account holder.

The money withdrawn must be used for college-related expenses: tuition, room, board, books, or transportation. The funds in the accounts are tax-sheltered. No taxes are paid as the funds grow. If the money is withdrawn before 2011 and used for qualified education expenses, the earnings are entirely free of federal taxes, although some states levy income taxes. After 2011, unless Congress steps in, the accounts are due to revert to their former status—with the funds growing tax deferred, but federal taxes due upon withdrawal. Even if taxes are owed on the earnings, the 529s are still a good deal.

Nearly all states offer these plans and each one is different. In some states, the savings are managed very conservatively, starting with a mixture of stocks and bonds for young children and gradually shifting to all fixed income before college. Others are more aggressive or offer a range of options. An excellent resource on 529s is *www.savingforcollege.com*, published by CPA Joseph F. Hurley, author of *The Best Way to Save For College: A Complete Guide to 529 Plans*.

How much can you save? Kristin Davis, an editor at *Kiplinger's* and author of *Financing College*, estimates that $100 invested each month at a 10 percent annual return over eighteen years would grow to about $45,000, after 27 percent federal taxes were paid each year. But if the earnings are tax free, those same contributions would be worth $60,500.

GIFTING GRANDPARENTS

COLLEGE SAVINGS PLANS give extra incentive to grandparents (or other relatives) who'd like to help underwrite the college education of their grandchildren. Anyone contributing to one of these plans gets a special break on the $11,000 annual gift exclusion. The law currently allows donors to put in $55,000 at once (by bunching up five years' worth of annual exclusions at one time) with no gift-tax consequences. So a husband and wife, assuming they could afford it, could together give $110,000 per child or grandchild—and start the account growing tax free sooner. They cannot gift any additional money to those individuals without tax consequence until the five years are over.

Golden Age of Philanthropy

It's not just family members who might benefit when you share your inheritance. Charities are hoping for some largesse as well. A study by the Social Welfare Research Institute at Boston College estimated that charities could receive as much as $6 to $25 trillion of the intergenerational wealth transfer during the first half of this century. Paul G. Schervish, director of the institute, proclaims, "A golden age of philanthropy is dawning."

Not only could the amount of money given to nonprofit organizations increase dramatically, but how donors give may change from past practices. This is not your father's charitable giving. Signs are emerging that baby boomers and Generation Xers prefer grass-roots organizations and private foundations over large traditional charities like United Way or the Red Cross. According to a report in the *New York Times* citing the Foundation Center in New York, the number of active foundations in the country rose from 40,000 in 1995 to 55,000 in 2001.

AM I A charity tightwad? When I spoke with Schervish, an expert on charitable giving who's interviewed multimillion-aires about their donating habits, I made a confession. I told him that despite my inheritance I still hadn't moved beyond a few hundred here and there for charity, rather than say a thousand now and then. It's not that I don't have the intent, I just don't know yet what kind of college expenses my kids will have, when (or if) my husband and I will retire, and whether we'll face health problems late in life without adequate insurance. Schervish reassured me I wasn't alone in feeling this way. He says most people need about $5 million before they feel financially secure and ready to give away sizable amounts.

Even if they want to do things differently from their parents, the charitably inclined need not strive to create something entirely new and different. "The real intractable human problems have been with us for a long time, and will continue to be so. Look for people who are working on that problem you care about," Barbara Kibbe, director of the Organizational Effectiveness and Philanthropy program at the Packard Foundation in Los Altos, California, told the *New York Times*.

If you're looking to contribute to charities within your city or region and need help narrowing your choices, community foundations can be a valuable resource. These foundations are organizations to benefit charities and people who live within a specific area, which can be as large as a state or as small as a city. Their job is to manage and distribute to charities—after carefully evaluating how well the charities are doing their jobs. Thus, they can be an excellent source of information on which charities are doing what and therefore on which are deserving of support.

Many financial institutions, including mutual fund management companies Fidelity, Schwab, and Vanguard, offer what are known as "donor-advised charitable funds." These can offer professional management and flexibility for donors with moderate to high charitable dollars (some accounts require a minimum of $10,000). Donors contribute to professionally run mutual fund pools, whose fees can be as low as .50 percent. Both the contributions and the earnings are tax free. Contributors, who get an immediate tax write-off when they invest, can make grants to any qualified nonprofit organization.

GIVING OR SAVING?

WHAT MOTIVATES AMERICANS to give to charity?

Some studies have shown that avoiding estate taxes is not the primary motive for charitable giving. A 1998 survey of affluent Americans by U.S. Trust found that their top reasons for donating were a desire to support worthwhile causes and a responsibility to share their good fortune.

When you begin thinking about donating to charity, remember: Not every charity deserves to exist. That's the plain-spoken assessment of Renata J. Rafferty, a philanthropy consultant and author of Don't Just Give It Away, who points out that the nonprofit sector is virtually unregulated. And while there have been scandals involving some high-profile groups such as such as United Way, Feed the Children, and the Red Cross, most of the waste is less obvious, like a leaky faucet. Some multimillion-dollar charities don't even have a business plan.

"What really goes on is waste, misgovernance and mis-stewardship," says Rafferty, that is often hidden by a "cloak of benevolence" or by people's fear of criticizing good works. She once resigned from a capital campaign project because there was no community support and the money raised should have gone elsewhere.

She offers these tips for choosing a charity:

- Don't be too trusting of every group that calls itself a charity.
- Examine the financial records. If an organization won't let you look at recent financial statements, this should be a red flag.
- Interview the leaders about the group's strategic plans. A good organization will welcome your questions and will also have a written strategic plan.
- Ask what kind of results can be expected and how they will be measured.
- Don't let yourself get forced into hasty year-end decisions.
- View your donation the way you would an investment. "If someone showed up at your door and asked you to buy a bond," says Rafferty, "you'd laugh at them."

Chapter 15

Heirworthy

With money in your pocket, you are wise, and you are handsome, and you sing well, too.
—Yiddish proverb

I t might take years, but at some point you will settle your parent's estate. That is not, however, the same thing as coming to terms with your inheritance and your family's legacy. Sadly, some heirs never do. In Chapter 10, Go Fish Finance 101, I compared receiving a bequest to inheriting someone else's clothing. The assets belonged to someone else and they don't necessarily fit you. You must adjust and alter to make a wardrobe that suits your needs.

Let me share a letter I received from a woman named Camille, whose father died unexpectedly in his sleep at age fifty-nine. She inherited about $100,000, which made a big difference to her: "It has changed our lives for the better. My husband is in the Navy and we got married when I was eighteen. We have three children and we had always lived paycheck to paycheck. I had recently gone back to community college and was only working three hours a day at an elementary school as a teacher's aide. When we got the money we paid off all of our bills and cars.

"We began to learn to invest, so we have money in the stock market and a small amount in an IRA. We have also put money in a CD and have some put away for the kids' education. We just got back from Canada so we've been able to travel more.

"The best part is that my daughter is now in a state college, and I go to a business university. Neither of us has had to take out a loan. Granted, I now work full time, but I'm confident that without that boost from the inheritance we would never have been able to get our heads above water long enough to get ahead. My husband will retire in two years from the Navy and we now have a nest egg that we can rely on to get us started.

"Life is full of unexpected turns. It's funny how they all turn out to be just the thing we need, when we need it."

Camille has reached a stage with her inheritance that I call "heirworthy." That's when you come to terms with the fact that fairly or unfairly you've been given something of value. That it's yours and you are worthy to have it. You recognize the true potential of your "inheritance venture capital" to improve your life and that of your loved ones. You might even feel empowered by your inheritance to make a big change in your life. You share it with family, friends, and charitable organizations. And, if all goes well, you will feel, like Camille, that everything turned out the way it was supposed to.

Struggle and Freedom

The time of life when many people receive inheritances, in their forties, fifties, and sixties, can be among the most happy and productive. Children are older and more independent and may have left home already, freeing up time and money for parents. There can be career fulfillment, as well as a time to enjoy what they've earned.

Middle age is also when many people come into their own as adults. Authors who write about the loss of parents during adulthood repeatedly note that these orphans feel an unexpected freedom at having to answer only to themselves. Some are emboldened to try new careers, to get divorced, to travel, or to do something they always longed to do.

Getting to that level of freedom can be especially hard for heirs who receive large inheritances. In their study of wealthy heirs, Paul G. Schervish and Andrew Herman of the Social Welfare Research Institute at Boston College found that some inheritors went through a metamorphosis they referred to as "liminality." In telling their life stories, the wealthy subjects dwelt on their struggles to overcome obstacles, and many spoke of relatively long periods in which they underwent profound change. Essentially, inheritors moved from having their wealth control them to having control over it.

Clearly, if you inherit a modest amount of money, your choices about how to incorporate it into your life will be limited. The more inheritance you receive, the greater your options, which can be both a blessing and a responsibility.

"Being wealthy gives us choices," says Valerie Jacobs, a San Diego inheritor and wealth counselor. She says that she is free to work and be productive, without having to earn money to support herself. "I'm doing exactly what I want to do. I love it."

ARE WE STEWARDS?

I'VE SOMETIMES HEARD it said that inheritors should strive to become good "stewards" of the money they receive. A steward, according to the dictionary, is someone who acts as an administrator of finances and resources for others. That is, not for themselves. And that concerns me. Is the money passing to you or through you? While some trusts might require inheritors to supervise assets for others, I think it's best for heirs to accept ownership and with it the responsibility to make the best use of their money. I've seen too many heirs paralyzed with fear about touching a bequest and using it productively—because it "belonged" to someone who is dead and really "should" be preserved for the next generation.

How will you know if you're heirworthy? Here are some of the ways you demonstrate that you're at ease with their your money and with yourself:

- You have recovered from feelings of guilt. Yes, your good fortune is the result of someone else dying, but everyone dies someday. You might have felt guilty, too, if your parents favored you over siblings. But you accept that you can't compensate for your parents' relationship with your siblings, although you can certainly try to reach out to them.

Inheritors can feel guilty, too, that they have so much when others have little or worry that society will judge them for "getting something for nothing." Try this little mental exercise: Imagine a friend or someone you like has received an inheritance similar to yours. Do you automatically think that person doesn't deserve it, shouldn't use it, or shouldn't enjoy it? No, you probably think, Well, that's fortunate. It's nice that David can relax for a while after he spent so long caring for his dying mother or, That will help Laura buy a bigger house for her large family. (Okay, well, maybe there's a tinge of jealousy if it's a larger bequest than yours.)

• Your assets are invested appropriately for you and your goals. After looking at your finances objectively (and probably with the help of an advisor), you develop a long-term plan. This can include selling off some assets you inherited—like a big block of IBM from dad—and reinvesting it for diversification. Instead of worrying whether that would upset your dad if he knew, you remind yourself that, like your father, you're doing what you think is best for your family's financial security.

• You have forgiven yourself for financial mistakes. Everyone makes mistakes and just about everyone makes mistakes with money. There are many smart, successful people in the world who don't have a clue how to manage their finances because they're too busy doing something else. If you need financial advice, go get it.

If you're struggling on your own, accept that you will make some mistakes as you learn. The hard part is to learn from them and not to overreact. Some people who invested aggressively in high-tech stocks in the 1990s that later crashed, for example, tried to make up their loses by investing even more aggressively. Others felt burned by the experience and vowed not to invest in the market again. In both cases, it's like shooting yourself in the foot and reloading. For some people, learning about finances is fun and interesting; for others, it's a big bore. The key to success for both types is to find a reliable advisor who will dispense the right amount of advice at the right time.

• You no longer seek approval to use your inheritance. While you might wonder what your mom or dad would think of your latest venture, you don't let their imagined disapproval hold sway over your life.

Cynthia, a high-level manager at a large Southern California social-services organization, says she spent her whole life trying unsuccessfully to win her dad's approval. He had wanted her to be a stay-at-home mom and felt that by keeping her management position she was depriving a man of a good job. "Even after he died, I was still trying," she says. Once both her parents died, she still didn't want to spend her inheritance on anything of which her father would have disapproved. But finally she began to spend according to her own needs and wishes: "I'm starting to get to know who I am and what I want versus what others think."

She remembers that her mother never spent money on herself. "I don't want to be stingy," Cynthia says. "That's not who I am. I think the 'me' is coming out. I'm fifty-five years old and I'm growing up."

MY FISH COMES IN!

IN CHAPTER 7, From the Grave, I described my conflicted feelings about whether to devote much effort to try to get my grandmother's Go Fish card game back on the market. I finally decided I didn't want to be swamped by my past. Did I want to be the Go Fish Heiress? Yes, of course. But more than that, I wanted to be the Go Fish Heiress, the author!

As it turns out, my fish could yet swim to market. I was contacted in 2001 by the son of the university professor whose students worked on my Go Fish marketing projecting. He was starting his own game company and asked if he could try to distribute it. I readily agreed. If you see any retro-looking smiling Go Fish cards at the store, chalk it up to a middling amount of perseverance by me, a lot of luck, and much hard work by Kevin Ronchetto of Fun and Gamz.

- You have some degree of control over your money. And you exercise that control. Even if your inheritance is managed by a trust and parceled out in portions, you still have control over what you do with it. At some point, you might be able to take control of the assets yourself.

  It's never too late. Financial advisor Candace Bahr

had a woman client who received income from a trust most of her life. But it was only at age seventy-five, eight years before her death, that she took control of it. Her joy at having her own money and being able to share it marked the final years of her life. She would take her women friends to lunch at the plush Ritz Carlton in Laguna Niguel and present each of them with a bracelet. She got a kick out of preparing her estate and named thirty-seven beneficiaries, including cousins, friends, charities, and her cleaning lady.

- You employ your inheritance to help set your course in life. John Levy, wealth consultant, says that inheriting can be a wonderful blessing: "It provides the inheritor opportunities to choose among career options, some of which may not be income producing. Being able to select a vocation in philanthropy, social service, teaching, or the arts is a wonderful privilege that wise parents can offer their children."

Mary, a nurse and HMO supervisor, says that her inheritance will allow her to retire early from her job and return to the kind of work she loved. In her present position, she rarely comes into contact with patients. Once she retires, she plans to do hands-on patient work, such as community nursing or maybe hospice: "I'm feeling I'm recalled back to my roots."

Attorney Mary Clarno recalls a couple who were comfortably middle class when the wife received an inheritance that she kept as separate property. "She structured a kind of dream life," recalls Clarno. The woman traveled frequently to live in a modest home she purchased in France. She also devoted time to deciding how to leave her separate estate to charities and family. Her husband, who was heavily involved in his work, was initially upset by her new life, but eventually became resigned to it. He even traveled to France with her at times.

In my mother's case, the inheritance she received from my father gave her financial security and the ability to enjoy life more. She was able to spend all summer, rather than just a few weeks, at the cabin on Lake Michigan, which she loved. Having a home in Michigan and one in El Paso kept her active in retirement and gave her a wide circle of friends. And when her health began failing, she was able to retire early, which probably prolonged her life.

- You are able to share your good fortune with family, friends, and others. Financial planner Joan Cudhea found her inheritance to be "totally life-changing," because she didn't have to worry about making a living day to day. She could do what she liked. And she could also give to worthy causes. "I'm able to be more generous," she says. "I have wealth to give away—in moderation."

- You enjoy your inheritance. Whether you get pleasure from the financial security it brings or the fun it provides by allowing you to travel around the world, your inheritance can bring you joy. Sue Ann, a musician, used the money her grandmother left her to help buy a sunny ranch-style home when she was first married. It's meant that her husband could be the main breadwinner and she could be at home with her children and work on music programs for children. "I've followed my bliss, my passion," she says. "I haven't worried about money."

A few months after my mother died, I went to see a well-respected, father figure–like counselor because I thought I knew what I wanted to do with my life, but was somehow frozen. I told him the inheritance would allow me to leave my job with a big company and establish myself as an independent writer working from home. I could more easily juggle working with taking care of two young sons. "Well, why don't you?" he asked.

I told him I was afraid—afraid I'd give up my job and never be able to go back if I wanted, of losing a career I'd liked and not being able to find another. There was also fear of failing, of losing my identity to mommyhood, and being consumed by volunteer work. "You are having a midlife crisis," he told me. I assured him that couldn't be so, because I wasn't contemplating an affair and had no desire to buy a small red sports car. But he was certain. And he was right.

It took me six more years to act on my dream, even though I would periodically hear his question in my head, "Well, why don't you?" Like Dorothy in the *Wizard of Oz,* I had had the power all the time. And that was scary.

Now, in retrospect, I see I also had a fear of stepping from an old familiar life into a new one, of growing away from the person I was when my mother died. It would mean moving beyond the time when my mother and I were together, when I consulted her on any important child-rearing matters, and when I could see in her eyes a measure of my life's progress.

It sometimes takes years to be ready to accept what the inheritance can do for you—to be ready, let's be frank, to find pleasure in your good fortune. Buying our home was the beginning for me. I remember walking into the downstairs bedroom with Rose, our real estate broker. Out of one window is a view of a lovely courtyard and the other looks over the lawn and up to where tall eucalyptus trees climb a hillside canyon. Rose asked if my older son might want to make it his room. No, I told her. "This is going to be my office. This," I said, pointing to the corner with a view out both windows, "is where I'm going to write my book."

Notes

Chapter 1

1. Robert B. Avery and Michael S. Rendall, "Estimating the Size and Distribution of Baby Boomers' Prospective Inheritances," American Statistical Association, Proceedings of the Social Statistics Section, 1993.

2. John J. Havens and Paul G. Schervish, "Millionaires and the Millennium: New Estimates of the Forthcoming Wealth Transfer and the Prospects for a Golden Age of Philanthropy," Social Welfare Research Institute, Boston College, October 19, 1999.

3. "The American Dream Reconsidered: The Hopes, Fears and Dreams of the American Affluent in the 1990s." Phoenix Duff & Phelps, January 1997.

4. Lutheran Brotherhood Reports, Lutheran Brotherhood, Minneapolis, January 23, 1998.

5. Robert K. Miller, Jr., and Stephen J. McNamee, eds., *Inheritance and Wealth in America* (New York: Plenum Press, 1998).

Notes

Chapter 3

1. Thomas J. Stanley and William D. Danko, *The Millionaire Next Door* (New York: Pocket Books, 1996).

2. Survey of eight hundred family-owned businesses, conducted by the University of Connecticut Family Business Program, available on its website, www.sba.uconn.edu/Family Business.

3. Arthur Andersen/MassMutual "American Family Business Survey," 1997.

4. Ernest Doud, Sr., "Unraveling the Mysteries of Family Owned Businesses," published on the USC Family Business Program website, www.marshall.usc.edu/entrepreneur/family business).

5. Timothy Habbershon, "Improving the Long-Run Survival of Family Firms," Wharton Family-Controlled Corp. Program.

Chapter 6

1. Paul G. Schervish and Andrew Herman, "Empowerment and Beneficence: Strategies of Living and Giving Among the Wealthy," Boston College, 1988.

2. John J. Levy, "Coping with Inherited Wealth," San Francisco, 1986.

3. David Bork, "Pride and Prejudice Against the Rich," *Family Business* magazine, Winter 1998.

4. Schervish and Herman, "Empowerment."

Chapter 10

1. Vanguard Funds advertisement, *New Yorker*, 2001.

2. "Tax Managed Mutual Funds and the Taxable Investor," KPMG Peat Marwick LLP, 1998.

3. Jeremy J. Siegel, *Stocks for the Long Run* (New York: McGraw Hill, 1998).

4. Allstate Financial Group, press release, Northbrook, Ill. January 10, 2002.

Chapter 11

1. DALBAR, Inc., Series on Personal Financial Advice, 1996.

Chapter 12

1. U.S. Trust Survey of Affluent Americans, New York, 1996.

2. Ibid.

3. Juliet B. Schor, *The Overspent American* (New York: Basic Books, 1998).

4. Ibid.

5. U.S. Trust Survey, 1996.

Index

Index